STRANGER IN THE MUSHROOM PATCH

Books by Amanda M. Thrasher

MISCHIEF IN THE MUSHROOM PATCH
A FAIRY MATCH IN THE MUSHROOM PATCH
SPIDER WEB SCRAMBLE: A MISCHIEF BOOK
CAPTAIN FIN
THE GREENLEE PROJECT
BITTER BETRAYAL
THE GHOST OF WHISPERING WILLOW
SADIE'S FAIRY TEA PARTY
THERE'S A GATOR UNDER MY BED!

STRANGER IN THE MUSHROOM PATCH

A MISCHIEF BOOK
#4

By Amanda M. Thrasher

Names, characters, businesses, places, events, and incidents portrayed in this book are either the products of the author's imagination or used in a fictitious manner. Any resemblance to actual persons, living or dead, or actual events, is purely coincidental.

No part of this publication may be reproduced, stored in a retrieval system, or transmitted in any form or by any means, electronic, mechanical, photocopying, recording, or otherwise, without the written permission of the publisher.

Text Copyright © 2022 by Amanda M. Thrasher
All rights reserved.

Published 2022 by Progressive Rising Phoenix Press, LLC
www.progressiverisingphoenix.com

ISBN: 978-1-950560-71-4

Printed in the U.S.A.

Edited by Jody Amato

Author photo: Jessica Prigg Murrah, Modern Studios Photography

Cover Artwork and Design, and Interior Illustrations
and Design by Kalpart.
Visit www.kalpart.com

*Dedicated to every little girl and boy who loves to use their imagination.
Enjoy!*

Contents

Chapter 1 ~ Mystery Invitation 1
Chapter 2 ~ Moss Bombs Equal Trouble 4
Chapter 3 ~ A Word to the Wise 23
Chapter 4 ~ I Can Jump Farther Than You 30
Chapter 5 ~ Oh No! 40
Chapter 6 ~ Make a Plan 47
Chapter 7 ~ Organized War 51
Chapter 8 ~ Safety First 57
Chapter 9 ~ Preparations 71
Chapter 10 ~ Let the Battle Begin 78
Chapter 11 ~ War 85
Chapter 12 ~ Oh, Dear! 96
Chapter 13 ~ Ellie 109
Chapter 14 ~ Follow the Fairy 122
Chapter 15 ~ Seek the Seekers 134
Chapter 16 ~ That's My Mommy! 141
Chapter 17 ~ Back to the Colony 153
Chapter 18 ~ Unbelievable 164
Chapter 19 ~ Emergency Meeting 174
Chapter 20 ~ Something About Ellie 183
Chapter 21 ~ Surprise 192

Chapter 1
Mystery Invitation

Lilly stared at her feet as she walked down the hallway. Deep in thought, she had no idea she was about to run into her friends. Rosie's sharp voice, asking Lilly what on earth she was doing, was a stern reminder to look where she was going. When asked if all was well, she threw up her tiny hands, shrugged her shoulders, and had no idea how to respond. When Lilly did reply, there was a noticeable amount of nervousness in her voice. Mademoiselle Francesca had sent for her during the dining hour, and that alone was very odd indeed.

"I'm not sure if all is well."

"I'm sure it's nothing," Pearle replied, trying to put Lilly's mind at ease. "It's not like you're Boris or Jack."

Pearle had a point. Unlike Boris or Jack, Lilly rarely did anything wrong, and if she did, it was typically by accident.

"Pearle is right," Rosie agreed. "Mademoiselle is probably going to assign a special task only you can do, and you can tell us all about it when you get back."

"Maybe," Lilly replied. "But what could I do that you can't?"

Lilly hugged her friends, straightened the wrinkles out of her sparkling pink dress, tossed her golden hair over her shoulders, and turned on her heels to walk away. Stopping herself midstride, she quickly spun back around.

"Shall we meet by the brook and sun our wings once Mademoiselle dismisses me?"

"What a fabulous idea, Lilly!" Rosie answered excitedly.

Pearle had an odd look on her face; they still had lessons to attend. "The brook, this afternoon?"

"Yes, sweet Pearle, remember?" Lilly giggled. "We have a free afternoon—a gift from the elders."

Pearle hadn't remembered, but the thought of basking in the sun aboard a lily pad for the rest of the afternoon while sunning her wings sounded lovely.

"How wonderful!" Pearle grinned. "I'm in."

Hovering two inches off the ground, *not three*, Lilly glided down the hall. Realizing she was hovering without permission, she stopped, lowered herself down, and walked the rest of the way. The day Lilly and the other fairlings could hover and fly at will couldn't come fast enough. It was no secret they were *all* counting down the days to sit for their flight exam. Once they passed the exam, they could hover and fly, in most areas, anytime they wanted. The thought of unsupervised flight was so exciting, Lilly forgot to be nervous for her meeting with Mademoiselle Francesca!

Chapter 2
Moss Bombs Equal Trouble

Monsieur Pierre caught a glimpse of Boris's arm in a midway forward motion in such a manner it could only mean one thing—a moss bomb was about to propel through the air toward a target, Jack. Boris and Jack's ongoing moss bomb war was notorious, but since The Fairy Games, specifically the Spider Web Scramble, Boris's quest to become the moss bomb champion was, no doubt, at his fingertips. Catching his star with his name etched on it and being pure of heart, Boris's wish had been granted. One wish—and of all things, he'd requested a never-ending supply of moss bombs! Having such a quantity of moss bombs on hand was becoming a problem. The situation was becoming detrimental. Everyone who found themselves in Boris's or Jack's vicinity got nailed. Anyone who had joined in the battle and found favor with Boris was well equipped with stinky moss bombs. Ivan and Zeraz were regular participants, and thanks to Boris, they never ran out of ammunition. No one was safe!

Monsieur Pierre appeared out of nowhere and stood behind Boris as he released a slimy bomb. He grabbed Boris by the scruff of his neck, but it was too late. Boris, dangling a foot off the ground, watched his moss bomb rip through the air and splat all over Jack. Stinky slimy moss ran down the left side of Jack's temple. Though Jack should have been expecting an attack, he'd momentarily let his guard down, and the stinky moss bomb took him by surprise. The sting forced Jack to yelp out loud and jump right out of his chair. His eyes searched the room for Boris. Monsieur Pierre, though he dared not say it out loud, recognized the skill it took to pull off such a sneak attack while dangling in midair. As soon as Jack spotted Boris's predicament and realized Boris had managed such a hit, he mumbled a compliment under his breath.

"Nice one, Boris."

Boris, a good-sized fairy, looked down at the floor he no longer touched with his feet and was reminded that Monsieur Pierre was quite strong indeed.

"How many times have you been told not to pelt moss bombs in the dining hall, Boris?"

Boris shrugged his shoulders. He wasn't trying to be rude; he honestly had no idea how many times he'd been told not to do it. He hadn't been keeping up and was trying to calculate how many times it had actually been.

"Whatever it is you're going to say, don't," Monsieur Pierre added as he set Boris back down on the ground with a loud thump. "I would confiscate them," Monsieur said as his eyes darted toward

Boris's pocket, where another moss bomb had already appeared and was ready to go, "but we all know there's no point!"

Monsieur Pierre's eyes rolled so far back in his head, Boris wasn't sure if they'd return to their sockets properly and couldn't stop staring at him to find out. Fortunately, they popped back into place, though Boris did notice that Monsieur had turned the odd shade of purple that he typically turned when he was frustrated or angry with him. Admittedly, the odd shade made Boris feel slightly nervous. Monsieur Pierre dabbed his brow with his handkerchief and mumbled under his breath, "*Your wish, my worst nightmare!*"

Monsieur stuffed the handkerchief back in his pocket. Boris thought about the advice that Lilly often gave him: *When in doubt, say nothing. NOTHING AT ALL.* He realized now might be a good time to follow it. Monsieur Pierre scolded Boris one last time and warned him not to throw moss bombs in the dining hall, and instantly disappeared. Boris wasn't often able to strike without Jack's knowledge, but with his never-ending supply of bombs, his skill and tactics were vastly improving.

Jack couldn't let his friend get away with such a fine hit and scraped off the slimy, smelly moss that slid down his face and set about devising a plan to retaliate. Wadding up the soggy mess into a tiny ball, Jack waited for the right moment to strike. Boris was on guard, knowing Jack wouldn't let a strike like that go. Fortunately for Boris, the dining hall was packed, and the chances of Jack getting caught were on his side. Taking a shot unnoticed wouldn't be easy. Jack picked up his tray, winked at Rosie, and moved to another table before she could say a word. Jack's eyes darted around the dining hall; Boris had moved too, strategically positioning himself between Pearle and Ivy, but unfortunately for Pearle, was still in Jack's line of sight. Jack's eyes darted between his friends, and just as Boris took a bite of fairy treacle, Jack's hand slid from underneath the table, and another moss bomb flew through the air and nailed

Boris right in the middle of his forehead. Perfect shot. Jack reached for another moss bomb while Boris tried to locate him.

"Jack!" Monsieur yelled at the top of his lungs, eyes darting from Jack to Boris wedged next to Pearle. "Stoooooop! Don't you dare throw that moss bomb."

Without hesitation, Monsieur Pierre appeared at Jack's side, grabbed him up and disappeared, only to reappear in front of Boris with Jack still dangling in his hands. Yanking Boris to his feet, he pointed to the door.

"You and you; my 'shroom, now!" And then Monsieur disappeared.

Sulkily Jack and Boris made their way to Monsieur Pierre's 'shroom. As they walked through the winding paths of the mushroom patch, they ran smack into Lilly.

"Hello, you two; where are you going?"

Jack looked down at the ground and kicked the dirt. Boris, about to open his mouth to speak, was shut down before he could a get a word out.

"Never mind, boys. I'm certain by the look on your faces you must have been summoned to the elder's 'shroom for something, likely trouble and moss-bomb related, I should think?"

"You would think right, Lilly," Boris replied. "But not one fairling was hurt during the hit."

Jack grinned and rubbed his temple. "Speak for yourself."

Lilly laid her tiny little hands neatly on her ruffled pink dress, and though she tried to bite her tongue, she couldn't help herself.

"Boris, when will you learn there's a time to listen, a time to eat, and a time to play?"

There was no point mentioning Jack; he'd never learn, and besides, he always pretended he wasn't listening when Lilly tried to help them. She wasn't trying to be bossy, but Jack said she could be a bossy fairy when she was trying to help.

"Well, good luck, then," she said softly. "I hope you can join us at the brook later; we're going to jump the lily pads and sun our wings."

Forcing her wings not to engage, Lilly continued on her way, leaving Boris and Jack wondering if they did indeed need luck on their side before they reached Monsieur's 'shroom. Though they walked as slow as their feet would carry them, it was inevitable: they finally arrived at Monsieur Pierre's 'shroom. They stood nervously outside the door, arguing about who would knock.

"You knock."

Jack shook his head. "No. You knock."

"No way. You do it," Boris whispered.

"Oh, for goodness' sake, you two, stop it!"

The door suddenly flew open all by itself, and Boris and Jack found themselves standing in front of Monsieur's desk. The elders' ways still managed to take the fairlings off-guard when they did things like that, plus it was a well-known fact that Boris feared Monsieur Pierre was reading his mind!

Patiently the boys waited for Monsieur Pierre to address them; they didn't have to wait long. Monsieur mopped his brow with his handkerchief, stuffed it into his pocket, and shook his head as he spoke to the boys.

"We knew this was going to be an issue, the never-ending stinky moss bomb request, but since you did earn and were granted your wish during the Spider Web Scramble, we have no choice but to deal with the consequences." He took a deep breath, and it was clear he was just getting started. "However, boys, it is imperative that we lay some ground rules regarding this annoying matter."

Ground rules sounded reasonable. Monsieur sat on the edge of his desk and stared at Boris right in the eye, then Jack, but didn't say anything. The silence was far worse than being scolded, and Boris nervously moved from one foot to the other. Jack stood as still as he possibly could, not daring to even glance at Boris for fear of cracking an accidental smile.

Hoping the moss bombs might need a moment to regenerate, Monsieur asked Boris to empty his pockets. Boris pulled moss bombs out of every pocket he had on his body, but no sooner had he finished laying them all on Monsieur's desk than Boris could feel his pockets filling up again! Boris dug his hands into his pockets and pulled out two more perfect moss bombs. Placing his hands back into his pockets, he retrieved two more; once again, his pockets were full. Boris nervously tried to shove the bombs down into his pockets, but it didn't matter how hard he tried, they wouldn't stay out of sight. Jack had no choice but to look at Boris and trying to contain his laughter was becoming impossible. He bit his cheek, his tongue, and even the side of his mouth, but no matter how hard he tried not to laugh, he could hold his chuckles no more.

"Oh, Jack, for fairy goodness' sake. It's not that funny!"

Monsieur Pierre snapped his fingers, and one of the stinky moss bombs appeared in the palm of his hand. It was a beauty, and the boys noticed Monsieur admiring the girth of the bomb, the stench that wafted off it, and the weight of it as it balanced in the palm of his hand, although they did wonder what he was about to do with it!

"I must say, Boris, I am surprised you haven't been in my 'shroom more often over these things." He held the magnificent stink bomb in front of Boris's nose. "Though they are fun one minute, they will get you in trouble the next." Passing the stink bomb in front of Jack's eyes, he continued, "You boys must learn there is a time and place for everything, sneak attacks included, and if you're clever, you can have fun and not end up in my office!"

Boris looked puzzled; did Monsieur say they could continue their war? Monsieur Pierre tossed the bomb into the air, Boris held his breath, and Jack cringed as Monsieur caught it with his other hand. Did Monsieur Pierre understand the power of the moss bomb? One wrong move and the bomb could explode all over his robes. Stinky slime would stick to Monsieur, and the smell would last for days. The look on the boys' faces made Monsieur grin. Did *they* not know he'd been throwing moss bombs for decades and decades?

"Jack, you almost nailed Pearle this morning." Monsieur leaned down and looked Jack straight in the eye. "Pearle, Jack. Little Pearle!"

Jack's eyes darted downward; that would have been bad, bombing Pearle unexpectedly in her chariot. Monsieur continued. If they kept throwing bombs in the dining hall, they would be banned from entering it at all!

"You'll have to eat outside, or in the wood 'shroom, or even in your dorm."

Jack didn't think that was a bad idea but figured he probably shouldn't express that and kept it to himself; the thought of eating anywhere but the dining hall was quite appealing. He loved the smell of wood in the wood 'shroom, and who didn't like to eat sitting on their bed? They were never allowed to do that; the dorm monitors would have a fairy fit!

"This is your last and final warning. Next time you throw stink bombs inside, you'll be assigned duties working in the dust factory, doling out fairy dust in the dust parlor, planting veggies, or even mining in the quarry."

Monsieur disappeared and reappeared behind his desk and sat down in his chair. He wasn't quite done, but the boys noticed his tone had softened.

"There are plenty of hours in the day to throw the bombs outside. Plan your attacks on your fairy free time when you're in the forest or the common area. You can enjoy your battles, sneak attacks, and stay out of trouble."

Having already spent time in the dust factory, Boris didn't want to be sent back there any time soon. Jack seemed unphased. Monsieur Pierre confiscated several moss bombs, dismissed the boys, and disappeared out of sight. He reappeared in the middle of the hallway leading to the elders' private study 'shrooms. The sound of footsteps bounced off the walls; someone was approaching. Disappearing, Monsieur Pierre reappeared behind an unsuspecting Monsieur Claude as he walked toward his private study 'shroom. Just as Monsieur Claude opened his door, Monsieur Pierre drew back his arm and threw one of Boris's confiscated moss bombs. It landed where Monsieur Pierre had intended, smack on the back of Monsieur Claude's head. The moss bomb exploded on contact, and a terrible stench filled the air. Green slime dripped down the back of Monsieur Claude's neck and onto his robes. Monsieur Pierre, unable to control his laughter, knew what to expect next. Dodging to the left and then to his right, he tried desperately to hide behind Mademoiselle Francesca, who had appeared in the middle of the hallway.

To Mademoiselle's surprise, Monsieur Claude pulled out a moss bomb and wheeled it across the hallway at Monsieur Pierre, who was now fleeing toward Liam, the foreman, who had appeared at the other end of the hall. The bomb skimmed Monsieur Pierre's temple but landed smack in the middle of Liam's face! Monsieur Pierre and Monsieur Claude stood in front of Liam, towels in hand to assist with the cleanup, but they couldn't stop laughing long enough to wipe up the mess. To their surprise, Liam pulled out two moss bombs from his waistcoat and smashed one over each of his friends' heads, just like an egg.

"Gentlemen, have you lost your minds?!"

The very question caused the three elders to burst out laughing. Monsieur Pierre, Monsieur Claude, and Liam, the foreman, were acting like a bunch of fairlings, reeking of something undesirable, standing dripping in slime in front of none other than Mademoiselle Francesca! Mademoiselle Francesca held her nose, shook her head, and wagged her fingers at all three of them.

"You're as bad as Boris and Jack. No, I take that back; you're far worse!"

Madame Louise appeared at Mademoiselle Francesca's side. The smell of multiple bombs released in one area simultaneously was almost too much to stand in such a confined space. The elders looked ridiculous, dripping in slime, and Madame

Louise found it hard not to laugh, though she tried not to since Mademoiselle Francesca didn't seem at all amused.

"I never once envisioned that Boris's wish would cause trouble for all of you as well as for him." Mademoiselle Francesca handed the three elders another towel. "Where on earth are you finding the moss bombs?" She looked the three up and down. "Surely you're not bartering with Boris!"

Mademoiselle spoke firmly, but between their rosy cheeks, soaked robes, and the terrible smell, she was having difficulty keeping a straight face herself.

"Monsieurs, that's not the example you should set for any fairling, let alone Boris and Jack."

Liam spoke up. "Mademoiselle, we promise we do not barter with Boris or any fairling. We come by these bombs fair and square."

Monsieur Pierre spoke up next. "And you are right, dear Mademoiselle—bartering with Boris, though a tempting idea, would send the wrong message. However, I will admit that when we confiscate the moss bombs, well, we save them because those are fair game!"

"For our bomb battles," added Liam, chuckling. "Boris's never-ending supply creates more bombs than the little chap knows what to do with, and he often sets them down, walks away, and forgets to come back to get them; those are easy pickings."

Liam held up a moss bomb. "These things are fun, and much like the Spider Web Scramble, they take us back to the days when we were fairlings ourselves." He stuffed the bomb back into his pocket. "You can join in our war if you like."

Mademoiselle Francesca managed a smile. "No thank you, gentlemen. But I appreciate the invite."

Mademoiselle tugged Madame Louise's sleeve, and the two disappeared into her study 'shroom. Moss bomb wars among the elders; what on earth would happen next?!

"Right then, back to our war!" chuckled Liam.

"You're on!" replied Monsieur Claude.

Chester, the special agent appointed to keep Lilly safe since she'd received the gift of sight, appeared out of thin air. Her newly acquired gift allowed her to see the special and secret agents that the other fairlings could not. Even some of the elders could not see all the agents, Madame Louise included, so Chester kept an eye on Lilly at all times. He stopped, read the faces of his colleagues, and without hesitation joined in pelting a bomb straight at Monsieur Claude's arm.

"You're all clearly up to no good. Whatever you're planning, count me in!"

"Moss bomb wars," Monsieur Pierre, Monsieur Claude, and Liam said in unison.

"Usual rules?" Chester asked.

"Yep, no invisible shots, meaning show yourselves during the shot. This does not apply while you're getting into position and, of course, no shots fired in front of the fairlings!"

The rules were reasonable, easy to follow, and everyone agreed on them. The elders loved their fun as much as the fairlings, and though the fairlings had no clue, they'd been playing this game for years.

Chapter 3
A Word to the Wise

Lilly stood silently and waited for Mademoiselle Francesca to speak. Knowing she hadn't done anything wrong, Lilly thought she most likely wasn't in trouble at all. However, that didn't make standing in front of the elder she admired most, Mademoiselle Francesca, any less intimidating. Out of the corner of her eye, Lilly spotted Madame Louise and Special Agent Chester seated on the left side of the room. Chester seemed to show up everywhere Lilly went these days, something she was becoming accustomed to since she'd acquired her unique gift of being able to see the special agents, protectors of the colonies, when others could not. Madame Louise smiled, and Chester winked at Lilly, which helped ease her nerves. Mademoiselle Francesca sat behind a large wooden desk. It was made of mahogany wood and polished to perfection. The reflection of her neatly placed scrolls bounced off the surface in such a way that Lilly could count each one, and Mademoiselle's inkwell looked as if the depth of ink was never-ending due to the reflection of the inkwell in the wood. Lilly expected nothing less from an elder she held in such high regard, but quickly forced herself to think back to the matter at hand. She'd been summoned! Mademoiselle smiled, and much to Lilly's relief, finally spoke.

"Lilly, dear, first and foremost, you haven't been summoned here because you are in trouble."

Lilly wasn't sure if she should speak now or keep quiet and not say anything at all. To her surprise, Mademoiselle Francesca turned to Special Agent Chester.

"Would you mind, Chester?"

"Not at all," he responded cheerfully.

Lilly turned her attention to her protector, who suddenly appeared from the corner of the room to stand right in front of her. He motioned for her to take a seat. Lilly sat down and waited to hear what Chester had to say, but it was hard to take her friend seriously at times, especially since he often tried to make her laugh. Trying not to grin, she focused on listening so she could please Mademoiselle Francesca.

"Well, Lilly, we have some news to share with you."

Lilly sat straight up in her chair to show that she was paying attention.

"During the Spider Web Scramble, you were informed that the colony and surrounding colonies were indeed on high alert."

Lilly nodded. She remembered spotting additional secret agents in the forest and throughout their colony, the mushroom patch. Her gift of sight, which came earlier than anyone had expected, allowed her to see the special agents when her friends could not. Even some elders struggled to see the agents, though they all knew when they were present. Chester continued.

"Though the threat has reduced significantly, and though we do not believe our colony is in immediate danger, parts of the forest could be unstable."

Lilly's bright blue eyes grew huge. Confused, she looked toward Mademoiselle for guidance.

"Yes, dear?" Mademoiselle Francesca asked.

"How can we be out of danger and yet possibly still be unsafe?"

Agent Chester calmly addressed Lilly again. "Great question. Be on guard at all times, but do not live in fear. Go about your business, your studies, flight school, and play with your friends. That said, if you suspect anything out of the ordinary or see something that makes you fearful, please tell an agent or an elder."

Chester walked to the other side of the room to stretch his legs, only to suddenly appear in front of

Lilly once more. Tapping her button nose, he grinned, and continued.

"We've had human sightings, but we're not alarmed—cautious, more like it. Humans are visiting the outskirts of the forest to enjoy the fresh air with their families. They like the area near the great waters."

Humans, Lilly thought, *so close! How isn't that a significant danger to the colony?!* Reading Lilly's face, Mademoiselle took over.

"Human presence will always be a threat, dear, and rightfully you've been taught to be alarmed when humans are nearby, and this keeps you safe. We don't want you to be alarmed, just aware, since extra security will be present in the colony." Mademoiselle took a sip of her tea. "Since you have the unique gift of sight and can see the extra security agents we have in place because of the unfortunate human presence, we're discussing this issue with you. This way you won't be alarmed, just alert."

"Boats," Chester added. "They enjoy their boats on the water on the far side of the forest. When the sunny season is over, they will retreat to their homes."

"Lilly, please continue to ignore the agents and never engage with them. If your gift had *not* come to light, we would not be having this discussion with you at all," Mademoiselle Francesca added.

Lilly understood it was important that her friends, especially Boris, Jack, Rosie, Ivy, and Pearle, didn't find out about her unique gift of sight. She had learned how to dodge Boris and Jack's questions, but Pearle was getting harder to mislead. Pearle often noticed Lilly staring at the agents or answering them when Lilly thought no one was watching her, and even Madame Louise was guilty of asking Lilly if they were present. *What are you staring at, Lilly?* or *Who are you talking to, Lilly?* were questions Pearle would often ask. Lilly felt guilty about misleading her friends but knew that she had no choice. Once she was able to tell them the truth, she knew they would understand.

"Well then, dear, we've taken up enough of your time. I'm certain you have plans with your friends. An afternoon without lessons is such a treat."

Lilly nodded. "Yes, Mademoiselle. We're going to meet at the babbling brook." Worried, she asked, "Is that all right during these times?"

Mademoiselle grasped Lilly's tiny hands in hers.

"Yes, dear. We're on alert, but we must continue to live our lives. Stay within the colony boundaries and, lucky for you and your friends, the brook is in a safe zone." She released Lilly's hands. "Please encourage Boris and Jack to throw as many of their moss bombs as they desire by the brook; it will cause them far less grief!"

Lilly smiled and opened her mouth to say goodbye, but before she could, Mademoiselle raised her hand, and Lilly found herself standing in the middle of the mushroom patch as her friends walked toward her!

Chapter 4
I Can Jump Farther Than You

It was a perfect afternoon, plenty of sunshine with a delicate breeze. Lilly and her friends lay on a giant lily pad in the middle of the brook and sunned their wings. The babbling water, lovely and cool, splashed droplets on them as it brushed against the floating pad. Though Lilly's friends couldn't see him, Chester sat in the trees above, watching the young fairlings play. Lilly's eyes met his; he signaled all was well, and without Rosie, Ivy, and Pearle's knowledge that he'd been there at all, Chester disappeared from Lilly's sight.

Boris and Jack joined the girls but had no intention of sunning their wings. Jumping from slippery rock to slippery rock, they tried to knock each other into the water. Every time Boris leaped to another spot, he dropped a moss bomb from his pocket, and Jack swooped down, scooped it up, and set it in an ever-growing pile he had on the side of the bank. Lilly whispered in Pearle's ear. Pearle giggled, turned to Rosie, and repeated what Lilly had said. Rosie, in turn, relayed the words to Ivy. Ivy cupped her tiny hand over her mouth to prevent her laughter from ringing out and echoing through the forest. If the boys asked questions, it would ruin everything.

"Who will retrieve the moss bombs?" Pearle whispered.

Lilly glanced at Jack's pile of moss bombs stacked neatly behind a large rock on the left side of the bank. Her plan would include the subtle retrieval of the bombs. Whispering once again to Pearle, Lilly passed along her idea. Each fairling gave Lilly's idea a fairy thumbs up.

"Ha! You almost slipped that time, Boris!" Jack hollered across the brook.

"But I didn't," Boris shouted back.

"Next time!" taunted Jack.

Lilly nudged Pearle. Pearle nudged Rosie, and Rosie nudged Ivy. The boys were still distracted; it was time for the first fairy to fly. Ivy sat up, stretched her arms, fluttered her wings, and stood on the lily pad. Hovering two inches off the lily pad, she proceeded to fly in a tiny circle around the girls before navigating toward the edge of the bank. In a swift dive toward the moss bombs, Ivy's tiny hand reached down toward Jack's pile and retrieved a sticky, smelly bomb. She flew a circle around the girls, lowered herself two inches off the lily pad, hovered, and made a perfect landing. Ivy sat back down, placing the bomb in between her crisscrossed legs, and covered it with her dress. Rosie flew toward the pile next. The boys were still challenging each other and hadn't even noticed Rosie had left the lily pad.

"Look how far I can jump; bet I can jump farther than you!"

"Is that a challenge?" Boris asked.

"Well, it is now," chuckled Jack.

Splashing cool water over his face and running his hands through his sandy brown hair, Jack looked at all the rocks and boulders near him. His eyes caught sight of one, the tip barely visible, peeking out of the water.

"That peak right there, sticking out of the water—betting two moss bombs I make that jump, and betting you can't!"

Boris rubbed his rumbling tummy, placed a hand over his eyes to keep the glare of the sun out, and tried to locate the rock that Jack had selected.

"What rock?" he hollered.

"To the right of the branches hanging in the water."

"It's barely visible." Boris grinned. "I accept your challenge; you're on!"

Rosie's wings began to flutter as she prepared to take her turn; being unnoticed by the boys was half the fun. Circling her friends, she dipped down and tapped each one playfully on top of their heads. Giggles filled the air as she flew toward Jack's moss bomb pile. Rosie checked over her shoulder; the boys were paying her no mind. She took the opportunity to swoop down and grab a moss bomb before shooting back toward the others. Pearle was next. As she flew toward the bank, Boris turned toward the girls and yelled.

"Hey!"

Pearle froze.

"Would you lot like to join our challenge?"

Pearle's wings disengaged, and she hovered above the brook, waiting to see what would happen next; fortunately, Lilly answered on their behalf.

"Thank you, Boris, but we're enjoying the sunshine and chatting about nothing in particular."

Boris rolled his eyes. *How boring*! The boys moved to another rock, and their challenge continued. Pearle engaged her wings, flew above Lilly, Rosie, and Ivy, watched as Jack lunged through the air, both arms and one leg extended, and by the tip of his toe barely landed on the rock. Jack was thrashing around, legs and arms flailing, as he tried to regain his balance. Boris burst out laughing and started a countdown, hoping Jack would fall into the brook.

"One a fairy, two a fairy..."

Jack beamed and, despite the water splashing around his feet, he managed to regain his balance and plant both feet on the rock. Taking a bow, he grinned and yelled out to Boris.

"Your turn, Boris. Crash and burn."

Pearle, slimy moss bomb in hand, nudged Lilly.

"Do you think Boris will make it?"

"It doesn't look good, Pearle. Boris isn't as agile as Jack, but I'd like to believe that he might make the jump."

Jack *was* agile. He could dart in and out of the tall grasses as if it were nothing, fly to the rafters with ease, and his speed and navigational skills were unmatched. Boris, loved by all, was a tad clumsy. He struggled with landings and departures most of the time, and his little round tummy often interfered with his balance. Boris took a deep breath and prepared to leap; all eyes were on him.

"No wings!" Jack taunted.

"I know," Boris yelled playfully.

Boris closed his eyes, took a deep breath, bent his knees, and started swinging both of his arms back and forth in such a manner that Jack could hold his laughter no longer. Boris, paying no attention to Jack, abruptly lunged forward toward the rock. Arms flapping around and legs moving as fast as they could in a running position, Boris bound through the air.

"Ahhhhhhhhhhhhhhhhhhhhh!" Boris screamed as he barreled through the air.

Jack's finger followed Boris as he flew past the rock and landed smack in the middle of the brook. Jack's laughter echoed all around them. Laughing so hard, Jack fell to his knees.

"Boris! Are you all right?" Lilly asked. "Grab my hand."

The girls pulled Boris to his feet, and Pearle handed him an oak leaf to dry his face. Jack managed to quit laughing long enough to ask Boris if he wanted to try again.

"No need, Jack," Boris replied. "I've already won."

"Boris, you missed the mark completely. That should automatically make me the winner."

Boris rubbed his little round tummy and, pointing to his legs knee-deep in the middle of the brook, he grinned.

"Nope! I didn't hit the target, Jack, but I believe the challenge was to see who could jump the farthest—was it not, Lilly?" Boris asked.

Lilly thought for a moment. Did Jack say hit the mark or jump the farthest? Lilly thought for a moment; if she wasn't mistaken, Jack had said both.

"Come to think of it, Jack, I think you did mention both distance and the mark."

Jack agreed. Boris was indeed the winner of the jumping challenge. Disappointed with the loss, Jack immediately challenged Boris again, but he made the rules clear this time. *Land on the designated mark.* Boris accepted the challenge. While the boys discussed their next landing target for the jump, Lilly discreetly flew back to the bank and lowered herself next to Jack's stash of bombs. Sliding one of the bombs under the hem of her pink sparkly dress, she waited a few moments before rejoining her friends.

"When shall we strike?" Rosie whispered.

"I think now is as good a time as any; they don't suspect a thing," Lilly answered. "On the third nod of my head, we'll fire away."

The girls flew slowly toward the boys, chatting so they wouldn't draw attention to themselves. Behind their backs, their tiny hands each held a slimy, stinky moss bomb. Waiting for Lilly's cue, the girls watched as the unsuspecting boys discussed their jumping object options. Lilly's golden curls bobbed back and forth as she delivered the signal. Once, twice, and when she nodded her head for the third and final time, the bombs whirled through the air toward Boris and Jack. Splat! Splat! Splat! Splat! The sound of bombs exploding as they hit Boris and Jack and drenching them in a slimy mess rang out. Jack spun around, lost his balance, and toppled into the brook, finding himself soaked through, just like Boris. Laughter rang out as the girls flew high into the trees.

"We've been bombed!" Boris blurted out in disbelief. "By them!"

Jack's eyes gleamed, pointing to the girls as he playfully taunted them.

"Great strategy, girls, you've proven to be worthy opponents." Draping an arm over Boris's shoulders, he added, "Welcome to our war, girls!"

Chapter 5
Oh No!

Chatter filled the hallway as the fairlings waited eagerly outside the carved wooden door to enter the great hall for morning announcements. Madame Louise stood in front of the massive doors instructing the talkative fairies to form a single line. Madame Charlotte hovered up and down the line, nudging those that stepped out of formation, so the line was perfectly straight and not crooked. Boris was grinning and staring upward at the ceiling. Madame Charlotte thought Jack must be hiding in the rafters; she was right.

"Jack, down, now!"

Before Madame Charlotte could scold him, the doors to the hall opened, and all the fairlings filed inside and took their seats. Mademoiselle Francesca, Monsieur Pierre, two senior elders, and two chief master engineers were seated on stage. Once the fairlings sat down, a senior elder, Monsieur Monroe, stood in front of the podium. He had long white hair, pale skin, and was quite tall for a fairy. His dark robe sparkled, and though he didn't know it, he lit up with such a glow it looked as if he'd been doused in fairy dust from head to toe two times over. Despite the early hour, his glowing robes were a sure sign that he'd already been busy all morning working on tasks and deeds for the day. Fairy dust clinging to the multiple layers he wore were a giveaway how long his list must be, and it was clear he had yet to stand in front of the dust blower to remove the excess dust.

Lilly hoped she'd be half as productive as the elders someday; they were always so helpful and busy. The amount of dust assigned to the elders was constant confirmation of the number of tasks they'd complete daily. Lilly and Boris knew all about the quantity of dust the elders were assigned from their time spent in the fairy dust factory. The manufacturing and production of fairy dust, an extensive process, were valuable experiences that neither Lilly nor Boris would ever forget!

"You may be seated," the elder instructed.

As soon as the shuffling of feet, wings, gowns, tunics, and robes had stopped, silence filled the hall, and the elder officially greeted them.

"Good morning. It's that time of year when our master engineers conduct their annual inspections of the mushrooms in preparation for the rainy season. Pre-treatment of the 'shrooms will follow, and any infected 'shrooms found during the inspection will be destroyed. Please, stay out of their way." Turning toward the Chief Master Engineer, he asked, "Is there anything you'd like to add?"

Unlike Monsieur Monroe, the Chief Master Engineer's skin was tanned and worn. He had deep harrowed lines that were forged in his brow, and round spectacles that sat on the tip of his nose. Shaking his head, he lifted his hand, and the announcements continued.

"Mushroom rot—nasty stuff," Boris whispered, and Jack agreed.

"It has been brought to my attention that a certain young fairling or two aren't complying with fairy rules."

Whispers quickly circulated around the hall. Even though the elder glanced around the room, Boris couldn't help but feel Monsieur Monroe was talking directly to him and Jack. Unfortunately, he was right.

"Not surprisingly, it has to do with a wish granted for unlimited moss bombs."

All heads turned toward Boris and Jack. Boris hung his head and tried to ignore the stares even though his cheeks felt as if they were on fire. He had, after all, promised to abide by Monsieur Pierre's rules, and he hated being the center of attention. Jack shrugged his shoulders and grinned. He didn't mind if the others stared at him; he simply stared back. He, too, had already promised and wasn't sure why their war was announcement-worthy, especially since Monsieur Pierre had already addressed the issue. The elder rustled his scroll, looked straight at the boys, and handed out a warning.

"Let's do better, boys, shall we?" He didn't wait for a response but continued with his announcements.

"Until further notice, fairlings are not permitted to fly near Lafayette Forest without supervision, regardless of their flight status; supervision is required."

"Oh no!" Jack whispered in disgust. "Lafayette is the ideal place for our moss bomb battle. Perfect place to execute sneak attacks!"

Boris agreed. Now where were they supposed to play without getting into trouble? Placing a finger to his lips, the elder shushed the fairlings. Explanations needed to be shared, and he wasn't through with his announcements yet.

"It's merely a precaution. Humans venture out this time of year, and human sightings mean preventive measures are put in place to protect the entire colony. We're not saying you can't enter the forest; simply fly with an elder or stay closer to home."

Lilly searched the great hall for Chester. She spotted him almost immediately sitting in the rafters, invisible to others but in plain sight to her. As soon as their eyes met, Lilly knew this conversation was like the one she'd had with Mademoiselle Francesca, Chester, and Madame Louise; the extra safety measures revolved around their discussion. Chester winked, but Lilly knew she could not react, as that would alert anyone else in the room that she could see him—or any of the other special agents present in the hall, for that matter. She felt safe knowing they were in good hands and knowing the elder had discussed the human sightings openly made her feel as if she wasn't keeping a secret.

"We'll be in trouble all the time now; I just know it!" Boris complained.

"No, you won't. We will be able to play in the forest," Lilly whispered. "We'll just fly with an elder."

"It won't be the same," Boris whined. "We'll constantly have someone watching what we're doing."

"It might work in our favor," Jack beamed.

"How do you figure that?" Boris asked.

"We could ask Monsieur Pierre to take us; he likes to throw moss bombs, and he could join our war and take our side."

Boris's face lit up. "If Monsieur joins our war, he'll likely want to fly to the forest every chance he gets. Fantastic idea, Jack!"

Jack felt pleased with himself. He never thought he'd like to have a teacher present all the time, but he just might have changed his mind!

Chapter 6
Make a Plan

Violet, Rosie, Dahlia, and Tori sat excitedly at the bottom of Lilly's bed and waited for her to return from the bathing room. They didn't have to wait long. Pearle's chariot clattering toward the dormitory, and giggles echoing down the hall, notified the girls Lilly was about to arrive. Ivy stood by the door, waiting to close it as soon as the girls entered the dorm. Madame Louise looked on but had yet to ask the fairies to climb into bed for final role-count. Lilly, as usual, was perched upon Pearle's lap. She'd forgotten her slippers and was trying to cover her cold toes with her nightgown. As soon as they entered the dorm, Madame Louise handed Lilly her slippers.

"Again, Lilly?"

Lilly blushed as she slid the slippers onto her feet. They were lovely and warm, and Lilly knew Madame must have put them by the fire for her. Grateful, Lilly blew a fairy kiss at Madame, who responded with a lovely smile.

"Hurry, little fairlings," Madame Louise instructed. "You have but a few minutes to visit before I tuck you in, conduct roll-count, and we get back to our story."

She pointed to Lilly's bed.

"It would appear you have company this evening."

Lilly hovered out of Pearle's lap and flew toward her friends. Knowing they shouldn't fly indoors, Pearle glanced at Madame Louise, who tried to hide her smile as she looked the other way. They had to make their impromptu visit quick, and Lilly wasted no time in making a complaint.

"I had to change my dress three times today," Lilly whispered. "I'm certain the wash monitor will pitch a fairy fit, and rightfully so, the next time I drop off a dress covered in slime."

The girls nodded, understanding her frustration. Boris and Jack were getting the best of them with their stinky, slimy moss bombs. They had already nailed Rosie, Ivy, and sweet little Pearle that morning. Dahlia and Tori, who were often caught in the crossfire, were also tired of being pelted.

"We have to devise a sneak attack," Lilly grumbled. "Practically all of my dresses are ruined!"

"I'm sure if we put our heads together, we can come up with one," Rosie grinned.

"Maybe we should ask Madame Louise to escort us to the forest. She still enjoys games and might help us plot a sneak attack against the boys," Lilly suggested.

"Plus, we could get extra tips for our flight exam," Pearle added.

"The boys won't know what hit them!" Rosie laughed. "We'll ask her first thing in the morning, before breakfast, because Madame is always in a good mood early in the morning."

A familiar sweet voice interrupted their chatter.

"Slippers under your bed, robes at the foot of your bed, and then you must all climb into bed. I'm going to tuck you in, kiss you goodnight, and then we can begin to read!"

Hovering to the center of the dorm, scroll in hand, Madame Louise added, "Aren't you just dying to find out what happens next?"

One by one, Madame Louise blew out each fairy's candle, pulled up their covers, kissed the top of their heads, and told them good night. As soon as Madame Louise recorded her count, she nestled in her chair, rolled out her scroll, and prepared to read.

"*Fairy Magic Gone Wrong.* Chapter seven; here we go!"

Chapter 7
Organized War

No matter how hard she tried to listen to Monsieur Bissett's fairy history lesson, Lilly's mind kept wandering. He was telling them about a battle that had taken place many moons ago between the East and West colonies that had led to an invaluable peace treaty; it was interesting enough, but planning a sneak attack was consuming Lilly's mind. Madame Louise had agreed to escort them to the forest during their fairy free time and had mentioned she was looking forward to joining the fight with the boys. *She must not realize how serious the war had become*, Lilly thought. Monsieur Bissett finally finished talking. To Lilly's relief, he raised his hands, dismissed the class, and disappeared. Fairies gathered up their scrolls and started to leave the 'shroom. Lilly stuffed her scroll, quill, and the spare ink bottle she always brought into her satchel and left with the others. As soon as she turned the corner, she felt a thud on the side of her head, followed by a disgusting stench as sticky slime slid down her face. She'd been bombed again! Her blond curly hair was stuck to her head, and her pink sparkly dress was dripping in stinky green slime. Uncontrollable laughter led directly to Boris, who was hiding behind the 'shroom door and, of course, Jack was standing at his side. Jack had his hand pressed firmly over his mouth, trying to hold back his laughter; it didn't work. Laughter spluttered through his fingers, forming the weirdest sound, until he could keep his laughter under control no longer. The sight of slime dripping from Lilly's head and landing, *splat,* on her shoes was too funny.

"Before you scold us, Lilly, we've been dismissed from our studies, we're not yet in the dorm, we're nowhere near the dining hall, and we're standing outside the class 'shroom," Boris managed to spit out in between his belly laughs.

"And don't forget you wanted to join our war," Jack added. "It was a legal hit."

Shocked, the boys didn't know what to think when Lilly burst out laughing as well. Was it a trick? Jack was right, they had joined the war. Another dress surely ruined; Lilly knew the girls had no choice. They would have to fight back sooner rather than later. It was time to gather as many stinky moss bombs for this ongoing battle as they possibly could.

"Watch this."

Before Lilly could say a word, Jack pulled a moss bomb from his pocket and smashed it on top of Boris's head. Boris caught the slime as it slipped off his belly and rubbed it in Jack's hair. All three of them were dripping in slime and stunk.

"Maybe we should add some more rules," Lilly suggested. "Look at us."

"No need for more rules," Boris laughed. "We've just got to be faster than Jack."

"Well, I have an idea!" Lilly grinned. "We could have an organized battle, preferably in the woods."

"Organized battle! What's that?" Jack asked.

Lilly explained her idea. Teams. Girls, boys, and the elders who would be escorting them, having a moss bomb war at a specific time and place rather than continual random attacks. Which, as she pointed out, were getting her in deep trouble with the wash monitor.

"I like it! We'll spread the word," offered Jack. "Maybe we can play, I mean go to war, as soon as our next extended free time."

"Maybe," Lilly replied. "But I'd like to state our demands if the girls win."

Jack glanced at Boris. *Demands. What could they possibly want?* Besides, how could the girls beat the boys, especially with Monsieur Pierre on their side?!

Boris shrugged his shoulders; he had no idea what they'd want and didn't think it possible they would win anyway. Let the girls ask for anything they wanted; it wouldn't matter.

"State your demands, and then we'll state ours," Jack responded.

"We have demands?" whispered Boris. "What are they?"

"I don't know. We just need to think of some because they have them," Jack grinned.

They agreed to meet in the fairy garden on the west side at the end of the day to discuss everyone's demands. Boris and Jack weren't worried; how could the girls possibly win with Monsieur Pierre on their team and access to a never-ending source of slimy moss bombs? They said their goodbyes, and even though the boys had not been given permission to use their transport skills, they simply disappeared right in front of Lilly. The girls wasted no time writing down their demands. If they were to defeat the boys, they would have earned the right to every one of them!

Chapter 8
Safety First

Fog covered the tall grasses at the edge of the meadow, making it impossible to see the forest treetops. Reports determined flight conditions were not ideal; fairies couldn't see more than two fairy lengths in front of themselves while flying, but the mist and fog made the conditions ideal for a moss bomb battle. Sitting on pins and needles, the fairies eagerly waited for permission to fly. Madame Louise gathered those she would be escorting around her; the girls listened intently, hoping for good news.

"Flight conditions are not ideal this morning—fog! If we go, I must insist we fly to Lafayette Forest attached to a fairy safety line. The fog will lift, but not for a little while longer. Any objections?"

No one objected; they were too excited the day would continue as planned.

"Fairy rule number one: safety first!"

One by one, the girls lined up without complaint, put on their safety harnesses, and waited for the fairy line to clip onto their safety harness. One by one the fairies were attached to each other and the line. Lilly and her friends couldn't help but laugh at each other; between the oversized goggles that covered much of their faces, harness, and line, they looked hilarious. Maybe they should wear them during the battle; hiding their identity might be a good thing.

"Did Jack or Boris say who was escorting them?" Madame Louise asked inquisitively.

"I believe they were to ask Monsieur Pierre or Monsieur Claude," Rosie replied.

Out of the corner of her eye, Lilly noticed Chester sitting on top of a branch. As soon as Ivy mentioned Monsieur Pierre's name, he started nodding frantically. Lilly knew Monsieur Pierre would be in the forest with Boris and Jack. Wondering if she should feel guilty for having this information, Lilly assured herself that it would be fine if she told no one else. Chester had disappeared by the time Lilly glanced back his way; no chance to request advice. She'd keep the information to herself. It was so comforting knowing Chester was always around, and Lilly knew he'd be back to check on her again soon.

Madame Louise tugged the line in front of each fairy. As each fairy fell forward, Madame Louise knew they were secure. Walking down the row of fairies and checking each one twice, Madame confirmed the girls were safely attached to the line and her. Excitedly, the fairlings hovered two inches off the ground, waited for Madame Louise's signal, and flew one behind the other across the tall grasses toward the forest. Barely being able to see was quite exhilarating and added to the overall excitement of the flight. Madame Louise knew the boys had not yet departed, allowing the girls to set up their moss bombs and hide in the forest before the boys' team arrived!

"Jack, come down from the rafters, and Boris, get your shoes on!"

Monsieur Pierre checked his pocket watch; they should have left already! He had agreed to give the girls a slight head start due to Boris having a never-ending supply of moss bombs, but he didn't want to give them too much time to take all the best spots.

"Who's joining us?" Monsieur asked.

"Sander, Dante, and Jasper." Jack darted down from the rafters and pointed toward the door. "There they are now. And whoever they told to come."

"The more, the merrier!" Monsieur remarked as the boys approached them. "We've got to go; we're losing our strategic upper hand."

Standing on the flight deck, Monsieur Pierre assessed the fog. It hadn't lifted, and visibility was an issue. He had no choice but to enforce the same safety measures as Madame Louise had insisted upon earlier. Monsieur Claude suddenly appeared amidst the boys and his friend, Monsieur Pierre. He asked them to save him a good spot, told them he was right behind them, and once again disappeared.

"Boys, pay attention, please," Monsieur Pierre addressed the boys. "The fog is dense. I have no choice but to implement additional safety measures, or we don't fly. Safety harnesses will be worn, and a safety line attached."

Boris and Jack scrunched up their faces in disgust. Safety harness; yuck! Monsieur Pierre remembered disliking flying on a line at their age as well. He decided to give the boys a choice, forcing them to make and be happy with their decision.

"I'm going to give you a choice. Fairy safety line, a nonstop fairy count until we arrive at our destination, or we don't go at all. Which one do you prefer?"

The boys knew without discussing what they'd prefer and, in unison, replied.

"Nonstop count until we arrive."

Monsieur pointed to Boris. "You start the line call as number one, and as soon as you hear Jasper, who is the last number in line, call out your number again. Any questions?"

There were none. Hovering two inches off the ground and signaling for the boys to do the same, Monsieur Claude pointed to Boris, and the count started. Their wings hummed and they took off.

"One," Boris hollered.

"Two," replied Jack.

"Three," continued Sander.

Followed by "four" from Dante.

"Five," the count continued.

As soon as Jasper called out his number, Boris started the count all over again.

Monsieur Pierre zigzagged over the tall grasses, listening to the count along the way until they reached the forest edge. One by one, the boys landed and stood excitedly in front of Monsieur Pierre. The fog was eerily dense; it didn't seem to be lifting at all, and the air was unusually still. So exciting! Did they arrive first, or were the girls already in the forest? The boys had no idea. Monsieur Pierre put a finger to his lips as he assessed the area. A crackling of leaves caused all their ears to perk up and listen. The babbling stream in the background sounded louder than usual, and when a bird started squawking, Boris nearly jumped out of his skin. Jack grabbed Boris's arm.

"It's nothing."

"Right. Got a fright!" Boris replied. "Something wrong with that bird. I think he sounded angry!"

Monsieur raised his arm and motioned for the boys to squat down and gather around him. The boys, who had moss bombs in hand, ready to attack, were on edge. Monsieur feared they were being watched and no doubt by the girls, but shouldn't they have flown deeper into the forest? he wondered.

"Tread lightly, stay close to me, keep your eyes and ears open, and move toward the underbrush."

They all nodded. Each time Boris stepped on a twig, it snapped, and everyone jumped, wondering if the sound had alerted the girls. Monsieur pointed toward a large boulder on the other side of the brook that ran through the forest. Hand gesturing that they fly, the boys hovered two inches off the ground, engaged their wings, and flew over the brook. Crouching behind the boulder, they waited for further instructions. Monsieur Pierre's ears perked up. He heard the usual sounds of water running in the brook, birds chirping from time to time, and rustling leaves each time the wind blew through the trees. Monsieur raised his hand, a stinky moss bomb sitting in his palm, and the boys did the same. Their eyes searched the forest, but nothing seemed out of the ordinary, though the feeling that engulfed them felt weird.

"Wouldn't Lilly's sparkly pink dress be easy to spot?" Boris whispered.

Jack grinned. "No, because she's a fairy, and hiding behind a clump of leaves would hide her sparkly dress. Plus, I bet she's wearing one of the splotchy green ones."

Boris's cheeks turned red. "Sometimes I forget we're so small."

They left their spot and zigzagged through the forest, boys trailing behind Monsieur, when suddenly something whizzed past Sander, almost hitting him. Stopping mid-step, Sander didn't know if he should holler for an assist or start pelting moss bombs in the direction of the moss bomb. He didn't have time to decide; they were under attack! The girls, strategically placed in the forest, had been watching them the whole time.

"Attack!" a familiar voice screamed.

"Attack!" Madame Louise repeated.

The boys were covered in stinky slime before they could tell where the pelted bombs were being thrown from. Monsieur Pierre gave the signal, and Boris set up behind a tree trunk. Pulling moss bomb after moss bomb out of his pocket, he compiled a huge supply for his friends. Monsieur and the boys loaded their pockets and filled their hands as they dodged behind trees, flew between branches, and pelted moss bombs back at the girls. Though they still couldn't see them, they could hear their giggles turn to full-fledged laughter.

"Got him!"

"Did you see that?"

"Keep firing, girls; we've got them surrounded."

Monsieur was well aware the last voice was that of Madame Louise. He could hear her but still couldn't see her. Ducking behind a boulder, Monsieur stopped throwing bombs and searched the branches above him. Out of the corner of his eye, he spotted Pearle. Purposely he declined to pelt her with a moss bomb; of all the fairies to spot first! He just couldn't do it. Pearle, on the other hand, kept pelting him on his back, his face, and his head.

Knowing the girls wouldn't leave Pearle unprotected, the boys continued to search the trees. Pearle never once stopped throwing moss bombs in their direction—brutal!

"Where did they get so many bombs?" Jack asked. "I thought we had the advantage."

"Boris leaves them everywhere, plus they fall out of his pockets," Sander replied. "I bet they follow Boris around and collect them."

"What?" Boris asked, surprised. "They fall out of my pockets?!"

There was no time to discuss the lost bombs; they were too busy dodging bombs flying toward them. They'd have to talk about it later. The girls' team's upper hand didn't stop their assault, and Monsieur Pierre knew he had made a mistake by giving them a head start. A massive black cloud headed their way, with too many bombs to count; they knew it was about to explode all over them.

"Run," commanded Monsieur Pierre. "Or fly, but move, now!"

There was no time to outrun the stinky slime cloud. Boris, Jack, Sander, Dante, Jasper, and Monsieur Pierre stood drenched from head to toe in stinky, slimy moss. The attack kept coming as they scrambled to their feet, held out their hands, and waited for Boris to hand them a moss bomb. Laughter rang through the treetops as the girls suddenly appeared all around them. Jack lifted an arm to throw a moss bomb at Ivy, but Monsieur grabbed his hand and stopped him.

"Let's call this a practice run, shall we, and we'll organize another battle and invite everyone back at the mushroom patch to play?"

"Monsieur," Madame Louise started to say but was laughing too hard. "Monsieur, that is a fabulous idea, but since we technically won today, the girls should be able to make their demands or request that specific ground rules are set in place for the next time."

"Agreed," Monsieur replied. "And I'm making a request on behalf of the boys: there will be no more head starts. You girls are more than capable of holding your own!"

The boys completely agreed with that statement and prepared to listen to the girls' demands. Lilly stepped forward, cleared her throat, and stated them.

"We'd like to request, nicer than demand, that unless there is an organized battle, the war doesn't exist, at least for the girls. Our dresses keep getting ruined, and the wash monitor is always upset with us."

"Not to mention it's hard to get the stinky slime out of our hair and makes straightening our wings nearly impossible," Ivy added.

Madame Louise nodded; she agreed. There should be organized battles; that way, the girls only ruined dresses designated for the moss bomb war. Not willing to accept defeat and making sure the first battle was documented as a practice round, Jack spoke.

"We'll agree to your terms if you agree this was a practice round and doesn't count."

Madame Louise looked upon her beautiful, though slimy, fairies and nodded her head. "Girls?"

The girls agreed; besides, they knew they'd won that round! Taking the boys by surprise and pelting them with more slime than they thought the girls could manage to possess was a win, plus they'd all had so much fun. No one worried how the boys worded it; it didn't matter anyway. They'd won that day and if the rules were in place and followed, they'd love to do it all over again.

"Then we all agree," Madame Louise announced. "We'll have another moss bomb battle, and we'll invite anyone who would like to join in." Smiling, she added, "I'm sure Broderick will even supply refreshments once the battle is over."

"Fabulous idea, Madame. Now, fairlings, how about baths and fairy snacks?" Monsieur suggested.

They flew back to the colony together, laughter and chatter trailing behind them, the girls once again connected by their safety line and harnesses, and the boys calling out their numbers. Safety first!

Chapter 9
Preparations

Preparations and strategizing for the next battle among the fairlings *and* elders took place all over the mushroom patch. Everyone wanted to be a part of the fun, although the elders tried to hide how excited they were in front of the fairlings. With the date set, scrambling to stockpile moss bombs had become the norm. Boris had become very popular, but he didn't seem to mind the extra attention, and Jack found all the fuss they were making over him quite entertaining.

"Extra custard to go with your fairy treacle pudding?" Cook asked.

Was that a real question? Boris wondered, nodding his head up and down. "Yes, please, and thank you."

Cook winked as she poured the steaming hot creamy custard on top of Boris's treacle pudding. Boris grinned from ear to ear. Fairy treacle was one of his favorites.

"Are you joining the battle tomorrow, Cook?" he asked.

"I think I might, Boris." Smiling, she added, "Fresh air, laughter, and good company sounds like fun for everyone!"

Boris pulled a giant moss bomb from his pocket. "Here ya go," he said. "This is a beauty." He handed it to her. "You'll need lots of these."

Boris was very generous with his never-ending supply of stinky moss bombs and finally caught on that he was dropping them out of his pockets and the elders were swiping them. Occasionally Boris dropped the slimy bombs on purpose; after all, *what's the point of a massive moss bomb battle if their opponents ran out of bombs too fast?* he thought.

Jack put his arm around Boris's shoulders and whispered in Boris's ear, "Do you think you might be able to barter moss bombs for easier lessons?"

"Nah." Boris shook his head. "I tried that, and can you believe I got fairy detention?"

Lilly, followed by Rosie, Pearle, and Ivy, joined Boris and Jack at their dining table. Without saying a word, Rosie slid her pudding toward Boris. Grinning from ear to ear, Boris dove right in. Rosie's reward for being so generous with her pudding was a big, juicy, stinky, slimy moss bomb. Surprised and grateful, Rosie thanked Boris.

"You don't have to give me a moss bomb but thank you. I know treacle pudding is your favorite, and I don't really like it."

"You're welcome, Rosie. I want you to have it; you girls are going to need it!"

Chester sat directly behind Lilly, out of sight of everyone except the fairling he was protecting. It pleased him how politely Lilly redirected the conversation to avoid anyone disclosing their tactical secrets for round two of the moss bomb war. She had the makings of being a great peacemaker one day, though Lilly did not realize it yet. Chester listened to the fairlings chat about Broderick's treats instead of the battle itself. Boris's comments made him laugh. *How could that fairling still think about food after fairy stew and two helpings of treacle pudding, one with extra custard?!*

"I hope Broderick makes his fabulous elderberry tarts." Boris rubbed his tummy. "I love those."

"You love all of Broderick's treats," Jack laughed.

"Yeah, but I love those the bestest!"

Boris reached into his pocket and pulled out a moss bomb.

"Would you like another bomb for your stockpile, girls?"

Lilly looked down at her lovely pink dress, with tiny specs of sparkling fairy dust clinging to the folds, and shook her head no.

"Thank you, Boris," Lilly replied. "But we don't have anywhere to put it."

"I can hold on to it for you if you like," Boris offered. "Give it back to you tomorrow, if I see you, that is."

Thrilled, Lilly knew they would need all the extra bombs they could get their hands on. She doubted they'd be as lucky as they were the first time, arriving first and picking the perfect hiding spots, and gratefully accepted Boris's kind offer.

They finished their supper, put away their trays, and said good night to each other. The girls headed toward their dormitories and the boys toward theirs. Jack couldn't wait to go to bed; the sooner he fell asleep, the sooner the sun would rise. Boris, on the other hand, didn't think he'd ever be able to fall asleep, too excited about the moss bomb battle, but he was wrong. As soon as his head hit the pillow, exhausted and with a full tummy, he was out!

Madame Louise and Mademoiselle Francesca gathered the girls around them before they tucked them in that night. They divided the girls into groups for the next day. Mademoiselle Francesca, Madame Louise, and Madame Charlotte would supervise each group for the battle, and though they didn't discuss it, they knew they'd likely each join in and play. Lilly, Rosie, Ivy, and Pearle had been assigned to Madame Louise's group, and they would leave at the crack of dawn. Excitedly the fairlings listened to their instructions as the elders discussed their plan one more time before they were tucked into bed.

"We'll rise before dawn and eat a light breakfast here in the dorm. As soon as the sun peeks, we'll fly." Mademoiselle Francesca pulled back the sheets on each bed as she spoke. "It may be difficult, little ones, but you must try to rest tonight; you will need all your strength for the fun tomorrow."

Lilly placed one of her moss-stained dresses at the bottom of her bed. The dress, now perfectly camouflaged with green stains, would be ideal in the forest. Mademoiselle Francesca looked at the dress and smiled.

"Perfect," she whispered, kissing Lilly on the forehead, before blowing out her bedside candle.

Mademoiselle Francesca walked down each row and kissed every fairy goodnight and tucked them in. As soon as the beautiful fairies snuggled under their blankets, she winked at Madame Louise and disappeared. Madame Louise sat down in her rocking chair, rolled out her scroll, and prepared to read.

"*Fairy Magic Gone Wrong!* I can hardly stand it. Can you?"

Lilly pulled her covers up to her chin. *Stay awake. Stay awake. Stay awake*, she told herself, but no sooner had Madame Louise started reading than Lilly fell fast asleep.

Chapter 10
Let the Battle Begin

Madame Louise pulled back the sleeping fairies' curtains, allowing the sunshine to pour into the room, and whispered into each of their ears to gently wake them up. Mademoiselle Francesca poured rosehip tea and placed a cup, along with a hot buttered croissant, on each bedside table. The smell of hot croissants wafted through the air, and soon the girls were sitting on the sides of their beds enjoying their breakfast and sipping their tea.

"We've taken the liberty of gathering all of your moss bombs, placed them in three large baskets, and have arranged to have them delivered to Broderick for safekeeping," Mademoiselle Francesca announced.

Squeals of excitement echoed through the dorm as the fairies scrambled to get dressed. Madame Louise walked them through the plan one last time, as Mademoiselle Francesca checked each one as present when they lined up at the door. The last thing she wanted to do was to leave someone behind accidentally; that would be dreadful. Lilly stood patiently in line; she'd had a terrible time preventing her wings from engaging because she was so excited, but Mademoiselle Francesca did not scold her for engaging her wings indoors. With perfect flying weather on their side, they were off to a great start.

"On three—not one, nor two, but three—we will hover to the main door. We'll fly in single file to Lafayette Forest. After we arrive, we'll retrieve our moss bomb supply from Broderick."

The humming sound of wings filled the corridors as they hovered toward the main door. As soon as they approached the door, it opened instantly, and they were on their way! The air was chilly but not cold, and the wind was light, truly perfect flying conditions. They flew toward the meadow and over the tall grasses until they reached the forest edge. Lilly was certain they must have arrived at the forest before Boris and Jack's group, since the sun had barely peeked over the horizon. They made their way toward the large oak, close to Broderick's house, as quickly as possible. Moss bomb battle rules stated each team must check in with Broderick first. Broderick had already prepared a picnic table filled with their favorite goodies for after the fun and, as usual, he would not disappoint.

Lilly noticed a plate and teacup sitting on the table with one or two crumbs scattered about, and she knew right away there was only one fairling who would eat two breakfasts, Boris! She was about to inquire to verify her theory, but Mademoiselle and Broderick were having a conversation. Verifying would have to wait!

"Everything looks spectacular, Broderick; thank you so much for preparing all these treats."

Broderick wrapped all of his arms around Mademoiselle Francesca. "It's my pleasure."

"I don't think I can wait; everything looks delicious," Madame Louise stated, eyeing the raspberry fairy tarts topped with cream.

"Broderick, it's lovely to see you," Lilly said as she hugged their friend. "The table looks amazing; you have all of our favorites."

Broderick beamed. "Thank you, Lilly, but I'm surprised you haven't mentioned my lime-green sweater. You usually comment on the color of my sweater each time we meet."

Lilly blushed. "It looks lovely on you; perfect color for a day in the forest during a moss bomb battle." She giggled. "Are you going to play?"

"No. Not today, not ever." Broderick smiled. "I'll stick to cooking; my eight legs might be a bit of a disadvantage for you all, don't you think?"

"You could be on our team," Lilly laughed. Pointing to the used plate, she had to ask. "Broderick, are the boys already in the forest?"

"Um. Well, um."

"It's all right, Broderick," Lilly commented. "You don't have to say anything. I know that's Boris's plate. No one else can eat two breakfasts before they fly into battle."

Mademoiselle Francesca clapped her hands, and everyone stopped talking.

"It appears the boys, or at least a group of them, Boris and Jack's team, are already in position. We must hurry and get into ours."

Madame Louise handed stinky green moss bombs to everyone. Hovering two inches off the ground, not three, they waited for Mademoiselle to give the signal. As soon as she raised her hand, they darted between the trees to find the perfect treetops. Perched on a branch, they looked as far as they could see into the forest below and the treetops next to them, but they couldn't see anything out of the ordinary. Mademoiselle winked and pointed to Ivy and Rosie; they knew what that meant. Proudly Ivy and Rosie flew two trees over, then made their way to the forest floor. Becoming decoys, they'd flush out the boys. Mademoiselle Francesca, Madame Louise, and the girls waited. Ivy and Rosie jumped from leaf to twig on the forest path, making as much noise as they possibly could and being deliberately obvious.

"Sssssh," Rosie whispered over her shoulder, hardly a whisper, and Ivy couldn't help but smile, knowing they intended for the boys to hear them.

"I'm trying to be as quiet as I can," Ivy responded, jumping on a dry crunchy leaf next to her. It crackled, and then she bounced on a fallen twig, and it snapped. "Sorry, trying to be ever so quiet."

As planned, a stinky, slimy moss bomb came whirling through the air and smacked Ivy right on the side of her head.

"Get 'em," Jack screamed.

One after the other, bombs pelted Ivy and Rosie. They didn't stand a chance, couldn't get one moss bomb off to nail the boys in retaliation, and the boys hadn't noticed they didn't seem to mind. Mademoiselle Francesca, Madame Louise, Lilly, and Pearle now knew precisely where Boris, Jack, and their friends must be. Chester, still observing from afar, desperately wanted to join in. Two more groups had arrived and were wandering around Lafayette Forest; it was about to be a full-on war!

Chapter 11
War

Moss bomb after moss bomb sailed through the air. The forest stunk as the slimy balls exploded on the designated, often moving, targets! A stinky, dirty mess complete with laughter, taunting, and directives from opposing teams could be heard for miles. Elders directed fairlings, fairlings directed each other, but *safe spots* were hard to find. Monsieur Pierre, Monsieur Claude, and Liam, the foreman, were caught up in a mini-battle between themselves. *If one suddenly arrived upon this scene, you'd never guess they were elders,* thought Mademoiselle Francesca as she dodged their moss bombs.

Chester flew from tree to tree, keeping an eye on Lilly's group, but couldn't resist joining in the fun and throwing a few moss bombs with the elders. It had been many moons since the elders had laughed so hard, and just like the fairlings as they darted from tree to tree, they headed deeper into the forest without realizing how far they were wandering. Chester, being on high alert, as were the other secret special agents, whispered in the elders' ears, encouraging them to take their groups back in the opposite direction, but no matter what they did, the battle kept drifting, as no one could be heard.

"Ahhhhh," screamed Boris. "That was a good one!"

Slime dripped down his face as his eyes searched the trees and thicket in every direction; he looked to his left, right, and above him into the treetops but couldn't see anyone.

"Over there," whispered Monsieur Pierre. "It's Madame Louise and Lilly."

Boris rolled up a juicy moss bomb, aimed, and threw it toward Madame Louise and Lilly, unsure of his actual target. To his horror, Mademoiselle Francesca popped up her head to assess the situation and his gigantic bomb smacked her right in the face. Ducking down as quickly as he could, Boris wondered if Mademoiselle Francesca had seen him. Monsieur Pierre burst out laughing when Boris nailed Mademoiselle Francesca and couldn't stop himself from nailing her a second time with another gigantic moss bomb!

Mademoiselle Francesca, Madame Louise, Lilly, Ivy, Pearle, and Rosie stood side by side and pelted moss bomb after moss bomb in Monsieur's direction. Covered from head to toe, Monsieur Pierre didn't stand a chance, despite Boris and Jack's help. Dripping with stinky, slimy moss, he ducked behind a large oak tree. Slinking along the forest floor on his belly, Jack tugged at Boris's shirt and pulled him down to the ground. They were surrounded by Mademoiselle Francesca, Madame Louise, Madame Charlotte, and the girls. Zander and Monsieur Claude were trapped behind a boulder, out of ammunition, and covered from head to toe in stinky slime. It was starting to look as if the girls had gotten the better of the boys yet again! Jack motioned toward a clump of trees located to the left of the boulder.

"Monsieur Claude is out of ammunition; we can toss bombs from there."

Boris nodded, and the boys stealthily made their way toward the clump of trees. Pearle, perched on a branch unknowingly next to Chester, spotted Boris and Jack. Darting toward the clump of trees, she hid in the branches. Jack and Boris sat in between two tree trunks. Pearle had a difficult time trying not to laugh, which would no doubt give away her position. Boris pulled bombs out of his pocket as fast as possible, handed them to Jack, who threw them to Zander, who passed them to Monsieur Claude. Pearle waited until he had thrown four bombs to

Zander and Monsieur before she pelted moss bombs on top of Jack and Boris's heads.

Lilly, spotting Pearle out of the corner of her eye, flew up and joined her. One by one, they threw the bombs without mercy. The boys were drenched and stinky! Monsieur Claude motioned for Boris and Jack to join him. Boris and Jack flew as fast as their wings could carry them and joined Monsieur Claude. Lilly and Pearle followed them. Hollering for backup, Madame Louise spotted the girls hovering above the water and shot off with Rosie and Ivy to assist finishing off the boys. Lilly landed on the other side of the brook and started throwing the moss bombs toward the boys as fast as she could. Chester, who was right behind her, tried to get Lilly's attention. Lilly refused to look in his direction, lost in the excitement of the game. Chester had no choice but to fly right next to her, where she'd not only hear him but see him as well. Going too deep into the forest was never a good idea, especially with high-level security warnings already in place, and they needed to all turn around.

Pearle followed Rosie, Ivy, and Madame Louise as they darted in and out between the trees; they were right on Monsieur Claude's trail. Each time Lilly was within reach, Pearle shot off in another direction. Lilly, having no idea of the urgency Chester felt to speak to her, kept flying with the others. Pearle stopped and raised a finger to her lips, silencing everyone. The boys were suddenly nowhere in sight. Everyone's ears perked up, listening for unusual sounds, twigs breaking underfoot, heavy breathing, whispers, or chuckles, but all they heard were the birds singing in the distance. Chester finally managed to catch up with Lilly and whisper in her ear.

"We're too far west, Lilly; it's time to venture back now. Remember, although everyone is having fun, safety first."

Lilly couldn't answer as she normally would since she was the only fairy present that could see Chester, and she was surrounded by her friends. Surely, they'd think she'd gone mad if she replied to *no one*. There wasn't an elder close by to assist Lilly with Chester's request, they were all too caught up in the game, but cleverly Lilly asked the group a question, knowing Chester would understand what she meant.

"Oh my! I just realized I'm hungry. Should we find the boys and head back toward the others?" Glancing at Chester, she added, "Aren't you hungry yet?"

"Come to think of it, I'm starving," giggled Pearle. "Broderick's fairy biscuits would be amazing right now."

A wink from Chester alerted Lilly that he knew she understood the seriousness of the situation. Madame Louise bent down and tapped Lilly on the nose. Beautiful little Lilly looked quite the sight. Instead of golden curls, she had slimy green hair, and her trademark sparkly dress had been replaced with a stained green mess covered in stinky moss. There wasn't a spot of pink on Lilly to be found anywhere. Very un-Lilly-like. Lilly looked awful!

"Such a clever fairy you are, and yes, you are right. It is getting late. We must gather the boys and head back toward Mademoiselle Francesca," Madame Louise responded. "And I can't wait for Broderick's fairy scone, jam, and cream. Yum!"

Madame flew up to an oak branch and looked around the area; she couldn't see Monsieur Claude or the boys. Holding her hands to her mouth, she yelled out Monsieur's name.

"Monsieur! Monsieur Claude, we should take the battle back toward the others; the sun will set soon."

Nothing. Silence filled the forest, as even the birds had quit singing. Though only Lilly could see him, Chester pointed to the west and shot off in that direction to find them and send them back.

"I think if we sit tight for a little bit, they'll realize no one is following them and head back toward us," Lilly offered.

Chester hadn't flown very far when suddenly a massive moss bomb came hurdling through the air. Chester dodged the moss bomb and called out to

Monsieur Claude. Monsieur Claude stepped out from behind a bush and raised his hands, queuing the boys to hold their fire. Acting as if he were surveying the area, Monsieur Claude had a conversation with Special Agent Chester. He agreed; time was getting away from them, and they all needed to get back.

"Boys, it's getting late. What say you we go back, find the girls, and head to Broderick's for treats?" Monsieur asked.

Boris jumped up first. "I'd say that's a fantastic idea! Especially since my tummy hasn't stopped rumbling in ages."

Worn out and ready for Broderick's refreshments, Lilly sat *crisscross applesauce* until Monsieur Claude showed up with his group. Chester swooped down next to her and whispered that it was time to go. Monsieur Pierre, dripping in slime, addressed everyone gathered.

"I'm out of ammunition and would love a cup of Broderick's rosehip tea and one of his fairy scones with jam and cream. You have all fought a wonderful battle today, all in good fun, and we'll do it again another day."

Madame Louise wiped slime away from her face; the smell was making her nauseous, and there was no escaping it. Her white hanky, now green, didn't seem to help, but she continued to dab at her face anyway. Declaring everyone winners, a tie between the two teams, went over well, not one complaint. Since they'd stopped playing, they realized how hungry and tired they all were.

Every fairy was counted and accounted for next to the giant oak tree. Groups were assembled for flight, and they prepared to fly to Broderick's for tea. Chester could already taste Broderick's fairy scones and cream. Every time they dodged a cluster of oaks and mulberry bushes, they were closer to sitting down for tea with Broderick. Just as they turned their last corner, the elders raised their hands, signaling everyone to stop mid-flight. Coming to a screeching halt, they ran into each other. Peeking around the elders, trying to figure out why they had stopped, the fairies wondered what had happened ahead. One glance and they wished they hadn't looked in the first place. A massive object, bigger than anything they'd ever encountered, blocked their path!

"Oh my!" Boris shrieked, turning white as a sheet and falling to the forest floor.

Jack, shocked at what he was looking at, didn't know whether to scream himself or help Boris. Frozen in fear, the fairlings waited for the elders to tell them what on earth they were supposed to do!

Chapter 12
Oh, Dear!

Lilly instinctively grabbed Pearle's hand, and although her mind told her to look for Chester, she couldn't take her eyes off the humongous object that stood before them. It was oddly pretty, in the weirdest, most obtrusive way. Strange. It had long, reddish brown hair, just like Rosie's, and the gigantic thing was wearing, of all things, a lovely big red bow. *A big red bow!* Lilly thought she had one just like it, smaller of course, in pink. The monster's clothing was simple enough, red on top and blue on the bottom, and it wore brown boots that laced up the front. Lilly quite liked those, even though they were very different from her pink shoes. Ruffled socks, all covered in leaves, peeked out over the boots. *How lovely*, Lilly thought. *I'd wear those.* For some reason, it was eating its fingers, a gigantic thumb stuck in its mouth; how strange! And if Lilly wasn't mistaken, it looked as if it might cry, of all things.

Chester appeared at Mademoiselle Francesca's side. It didn't take them long to assess that the monster was a young one. Lilly, being the only fairling that could see Chester, wondered what he was discussing with the elders. Suddenly Boris came to and popped his head up; the timing couldn't have been worse! He took one look at the monster and screamed as loud as he could.

"Ahhhhhhhhhhhhhh . . . there's a human!"

Human, thought Lilly, *why didn't I think of that?* Boris's claim made total sense. It had fingers, and she assumed toes, eyes, mouth, and a nose. Lilly had never seen a human up close before; it certainly wasn't what she expected.

"It's a human child," Monsieur Pierre whispered to the boys. "She's not fully grown, much like you. She's like a fairling, only much bigger."

Jack wrapped his hands around Boris's mouth. "Quit yelling; it might see us."

Boris peeled Jack's hands away and whispered, "You mean it hasn't already?"

"I'm not sure," Jack replied. "But we'll know soon enough."

Chester pulled Mademoiselle toward a clump of bushes next to a boulder by the edge of the water, and then guided everyone else slowly toward that spot. One by one, they ducked under the bushes and waited. The ground started to shake and, to their horror, the human child pulled herself to her feet and walked toward the clump of bushes.

"Hi."

It spoke.

"Oh, dear!" Mademoiselle Francesca whispered frantically. "It's seen us."

"Hi," the voice echoed again. "Hi, little person."

Her voice sounded funny. It was loud and had a weird sound to it. She sounded like she was talking with a mouthful of fairy gumballs.

"What should we do?" Madame Louise asked frantically, grabbing Mademoiselle Francesca by the arm. "It's seen us."

Mademoiselle Francesca gingerly took a step toward the human, but Monsieur Pierre grabbed her arm, worried something terrible might happen to her.

"I'll go," he offered.

Mademoiselle Francesca shook her head. "Thank you, Monsieur, but since we've established it must be a child, I think she may need a softer approach."

Chester and the other agents nodded; sending Mademoiselle was the right thing to do. They needed to know why the child was in the forest alone. Where were her humans? They would be terrified once they realized she was missing. Or worse, they might be close by! Nervously, Mademoiselle Francesca hovered two inches off the ground, always a pro, engaged her wings, and flew up to eye level with the human to talk to her away from the others.

"Hello, dear. I'm Mademoiselle Francesca."

The little one had big brown eyes to match her brown hair, rosy cheeks, dimples, and a sweet smile that practically covered her whole face. She reached out and tried to grab Mademoiselle mid-flight, but Mademoiselle Francesca was faster than the human and darted out of her grasp. Knowing she was so young, Mademoiselle addressed her as if she were one of her fairlings.

"You are big and I am small, yet I am much older than you." Mademoiselle Francesca smiled sweetly at the little one and spoke kindly. "If you grab me, you will accidentally hurt me, so please don't try to snatch me up in your hands."

She circled the human, hiding her concern. "You are a human, a little child, but I am an elder fairy. My name is Mademoiselle Francesca. What's your name?"

The little girl smiled and pointed at her coveralls. "I've got new coveralls."

Mademoiselle nodded. "They're very nice. What's your name?"

"Ellie. My name is Ellie."

"Nice to meet you. Ellie, where are your elders?"

Ellie looked puzzled. What was an elder? Chester softly whispered in Mademoiselle's ear; the fairlings and elders, not sure what on earth to think, looked on.

"Ah, yes, you're right," whispered Mademoiselle under her breath. "Thank you so much, Chester."

"Parents, dear. Where are your mommy and daddy?"

Ellie plopped down on the ground, the ground shook the fairies, and held up her hands in dismay. Analyzing Mademoiselle, as if trying to identify what sort of creature, person, or thing Mademoiselle was, it took her a moment to answer. Finally, with a pouty lip, Ellie responded.

"Where's my momma?"

Lilly softened her grip on Pearle's hand.

"What a lovely name," Lilly whispered. "I thought she'd be scarier, being human and all, didn't you?"

"Me too," Pearle replied.

"I know we're supposed to be cautious and leery of humans, but somehow I don't feel afraid."

Boris couldn't believe what he was hearing. His eyes grew huge, and his voice elevated to the strangest pitch Lilly had ever heard.

"Lilly, have you gone mad?! Look at the size of that thing!"

"She's not a thing, Boris. She's a human. A little human."

Boris spoke with such distress in his voice that Monsieur Pierre had to intervene.

"You are right to remain alarmed when you see or hear of a human in our vicinity. They're dangerous to our existence, and that will never change. However, there are exceptions to every rule, and this may be one of those times." Monsieur Pierre pointed to Ellie. "Children, I believe they're called, are young humans just like you're a young fairling. I can assure you, in many ways, she's quite helpless at the moment."

Jack wasn't buying it and couldn't take his eyes off Ellie. If this was a little human, he didn't ever want to cross paths with a full-grown one!

The elders had a problem. They couldn't leave the child alone in the forest; it was too dangerous. Knowing her humans would be searching for her created a treacherous situation for them and the colony. Madame Louise offered to distract the child while the elders figured out a plan. Flying in front of Ellie, Madame Louise introduced herself. Madame's voice was shaky, and her hands were trembling. Even though this was a child, she was terrified.

A tug on Mademoiselle Francesca's skirt alerted her that someone was by her side. Looking down, she saw Lilly standing next to her. Surprised, she asked Lilly what was wrong.

"Nothing, Mademoiselle. I was wondering if I may join Madame Louise."

"That's not a good idea, Lilly. I'm afraid it's far too dangerous," Mademoiselle Francesca replied. "But I'm grateful that you offered. What a brave little fairy you are!"

Ellie, aware her parents were nowhere in sight, suddenly felt afraid. Her eyes filled to the brim with tears. Her face scrunched up, and an awful sound left her mouth as great big tears poured down her face. The unusual sound was terrifying, loud, and scary to the fairlings. Boris half jumped out of his skin. Lilly tugged at Mademoiselle's skirt again. Mademoiselle, against her better judgment, wondered if a fairy could be the answer to comforting the child. With reservation, and Chester by Lilly's side, Mademoiselle agreed to let Lilly fly with Madame Louise to try to comfort Ellie.

"Not too close, Lilly. I don't like it. You must take every precaution that Chester asks of you."

Lilly nodded and flew to Madame Louise, who introduced her to Ellie. Ellie stopped sobbing as she stared at the tiny thing flapping around her. She could hardly believe her eyes: a tinier fairy than the ones she'd just seen. Ellie reached out her hand to grab Lilly, but Chester, quick as lightening, pulled Lilly out of the way, avoiding Ellie's grasp. Ellie's curiosity could accidentally hurt a tiny fairy. Lilly, for reasons she could not explain, still did not feel afraid. Her heart felt sad for Ellie, who wore one lone teardrop on her rosy cheek.

"Hello, Ellie. My name is Lilly."

Ellie's face scrunched up again, and she pinched her nose.

"Lilly, you smell bad."

Lilly looked down at her slimy, stinky, green, moss-covered dress and had to laugh at herself. "You're right; I stink."

Ellie managed a tiny smile and asked Lilly why she was so small, and how she could fly.

"I'm a fairy," Lilly responded proudly. "All fairies have wings."

"I don't have any wings."

"But you're not a fairy," Lilly replied with a great big smile. "But you do have two arms like me, two hands, ten fingers, two legs, two feet, ten toes, I think, and even a button nose."

Ellie started to feel better; at least she wasn't alone. Lilly's tummy rumbled, reminding her she hadn't eaten anything since early morning, and she was hungry. Boris must be starving, and she was certain Broderick would notice they hadn't yet arrived for tea. He would be worried. Ellie must be getting hungry too, thought Lilly, since, with the exception of their size and wings, they seemed very much alike.

"Madame Louise," Lilly whispered.

"Yes, dear?"

"Do you think Broderick will send out a search party once he realizes we haven't arrived for tea?"

Madame Louise pondered the question.

"Lilly, I do think he might alert the others." She hesitated before adding, "Unless the agents alerted him of our predicament. Either way, I think help may arrive soon."

Chester had put out an emergency alert, and agents were searching the area for Ellie's parents. As fast as they could, the agents had flown to the water's edge on the other side of the forest; humans were often spotted by the water. The elders knew that as dangerous as it was, they needed to protect the child and keep their fairlings safe. Putting their heads together, they devised a plan. They would escort the child back into the forest, leave her in a safe spot where her humans would find her, and allow them to reunite. Surely Ellie would be unable to describe what she had witnessed. Protecting the colony from a child's words was a genuine concern. The priority shifted from worrying about things they couldn't control to reuniting her with her mommy and daddy.

Special Agent Arley suddenly appeared; he had an update. The humans had been found on the east side of the forest and, as expected, were frantically looking for Ellie. They had put together a search party and were headed west in their direction. They had to move fast; the farther they took the child east, the safer they would be.

"It appears the young one was with her siblings, two older brothers, when she wandered off. It's terribly sad, because they're blaming themselves." He hung his head. "I felt awful that I couldn't tell them not to worry, that she was safe, but the risk was too great."

Mademoiselle Francesca nodded; she understood. Glancing at Lilly chatting with the child, she said, "For everyone's sake, we must reunite them as soon as possible."

Time was of the essence. Fingers crossed, they could lead the child to the humans by nightfall, but in order to pull it off, everyone would have to work together.

Chapter 13
Ellie

Between worrying about Ellie, the constant complaining of itchy skin and terrible smell, not to mention how hideous everyone looked dripping in slime, Mademoiselle Francesca couldn't take it anymore! Combining the fairy dust she had left with what the other elders had brought with them, she sprinkled fairy dust all over the fairlings. A snap of her fingers and, just like that, even Lilly's moss-stained dress was sparkly clean again.

"There, that's better," Mademoiselle Francesca stated. "At least we're now presentable for our young stranger, and we aren't nearly as offensive to her sense of smell."

Ellie watched Lilly balance on the tip of her elbow. Why were fairies so little? Ellie didn't know, but watching the now-clean Lilly in what looked like a brand-new sparkly pink dress was fun and kept her mind off her mommy.

"You look like a princess, a fairy princess," Ellie whispered. "I like the sparkles on your dress."

Lilly spun around. "Thank you, Ellie. Pink is my favorite color, and just about everything I wear is a shade of pink."

"What's your favorite color?" Lilly asked.

"Red," she said immediately. "I like the color red."

"Like your bow," smiled Lilly.

A loud gurgling noise came from Ellie's tummy, just like Lilly's rumble, but much louder. Everyone turned and stared. Ellie rubbed her tummy, and it occurred to Mademoiselle the child likely hadn't eaten in a while. Mademoiselle pulled Agent Arley aside and whispered in his ear. Agent Arley nodded, signaling his approval. Mademoiselle instructed Madame Louise to help watch over Lilly while the elders watched over the fairlings, and then Mademoiselle disappeared. Jack, observing the situation, nudged Boris.

"The elders were talking; if Ellie's parents do not find her soon, the situation for everyone will become precarious."

"What do they mean by precarious?"

"I think it means dangerous, Boris. Dangerous for everyone."

Boris kept his eyes on Lilly. Lilly certainly was brave, dancing and singing to stop Ellie from crying. She could become a squashed fairy at any given moment. Shuddering at the thought, Boris kept a watchful eye on his friend.

Each time Lilly's wings engaged and fluttered, specs of fairy dust fell. Ellie tried to catch the sparkling dust, but every time she tried to grab it, it slipped through her fingers. The sparkling specks shone in the dimming sunlight; they were beautiful and made Ellie smile. Lilly had no idea she was dropping dust; it was for the best. She would have been upset with herself had she known fairy dust was being wasted. Ellie turned toward Boris and, to his horror, made perfect eye contact.

"Ahhhhh!" Boris squawked, visibly shaken. *"She's looking at us!"*

Ellie placed her hand on the ground, inviting Boris to come and play with them, but Boris couldn't move. Fear held his feet in one place. Monsieur Claude swooped down onto the palm of Ellie's hand, tickled it, and darted upwards as fast as he could. Ellie tightly clenched her fist, giggles echoed throughout the forest, and she completely forgot about Boris. Jack's curiosity about the human child was intensifying. *Humans were dangerous and threatened their very existence, yet here sat one, playing with Lilly, and as big as it was, it didn't look terrifying at all.* He inched toward Ellie. Boris grabbed his arm, stopping him from making the biggest mistake of his life.

"Jack, noooooooo!"

"I'd like to meet her." Jack hovered off the ground and pulled Boris to his feet. "Come on; it will be fine. Look, Lilly is still playing with her."

Boris hesitated but slowly stood up and hovered three, not his required two, inches off the ground.

"You first, mate."

Jack took the lead and flew closer to Ellie, hovering next to Monsieur Claude and Rosie. Shockingly, Boris was at his side. Monsieur Claude nodded, indicating all was well and allowed the boys to inch a little closer. If they weren't afraid, they could assist Lilly with distracting Ellie while the elders executed their plan. Hungry, Ellie's tummy rumbled again. It was loud and echoed all around them.

"She growled at me!" Boris snapped. "Did you hear that? She growled right at me!"

Lilly hovered next to Boris, assuring him that Ellie would not eat him. She was just hungry. Boris was starving and then understood why her tummy made such a terrible noise. Jack couldn't stop staring at her feet; they were humongous. One wrong step, and they'd all be flattened. His fairy life suddenly flashed before his eyes and, although usually fearless, Jack suddenly felt quite ill. Becoming restless, Ellie pulled herself to her feet. Her strength, even as a child, could overcome the elders. Agent Arley, Chester, Monsieur Claude, and Monsieur Pierre flew as fast as they could and held up their hands in front of Ellie.

"Stop, please!" demanded Agent Arley.

The last thing they needed was for Ellie to wander deeper into the forest until they were ready. The situation was already dire. Ellie wasn't sure if she should laugh or cry. The fairy man was funny looking, seemed a tad angry, and had startled her, but now she was reminded she missed her mommy. Her face started to twist up, and Ellie had to work hard to fight back her tears. Out of fairy dust and unsure what to do to comfort the child, Agent Arley reached out to Lilly.

"Fix her."

"Fix her?" Lilly asked. "How?"

Agent Arley shrugged his shoulders. Babysitting a human wasn't a task he felt equipped to handle, but Lilly had been amazing so far.

"Play a game, anything to keep her here in this spot until we're ready to move."

"Ellie, would you like to play *I spy with my little fairy eye*?"

Ellie nodded her head, but her grumbling tummy let everyone know how hungry she was.

"Can I have a snack?"

"What's a snack?" Lilly whispered to Rosie.

"I think a fairy treat." She flew toward the elders. "I'll ask Madame Louise."

"She's hungry. You're right. I imagine it must be like a fairy treat." Madame Louise shook her head. "Lost and hungry—terrible combination."

Ellie plopped back down and leaned against a large oak tree. She held out the palm of her hand and motioned for Lilly. Pearle and Rosie hovered next to

Ellie's elbow. Pearle frantically wagged her finger, hoping Lilly would agree that landing on the human's hand was a terrible idea. Chester instructed Lilly to ask Ellie to turn her hand over. If she were going to land on the human's hand, it was going to be in such a way she couldn't be trapped in the child's grasp. Warning Lilly to be careful, Chester thought Mademoiselle Francesca would have his head if she could see what Lilly was about to do. Lilly put a hand on her tiny hip and pointed a finger playfully at Ellie.

"I'll land on your hand if you promise to turn your hand over. Like this." Lilly demonstrated. "This way, I'm landing on the back of your hand; it's flatter, easier for landing." *And harder to clench your hand closed with me trapped in it.* Lilly smiled, and her big blue eyes sparkled.

"Do you agree, Ellie?"

Ellie nodded. "I agree."

"Pinky-fairy swear?"

Ellie nodded, turned over her hand, and held out the pinky finger on her other hand. Though it was impossible to link fingers, Lilly and Ellie touched their pinky tippy tips together.

"I pinky-fairy swear," Ellie said.

Boris couldn't look. Head down, he stood behind Jack and waited to see if the giant human would squash his dear friend. Lilly slowly hovered over Ellie's hand, and Chester remained by her side as she lowered herself down. As soon as her tiny feet touched down on Ellie's skin, Ellie giggled out loud. Rosie gasped, but Ellie managed to hold her little hand steady. Rosie and Pearle joined Lilly on the back of Ellie's hand. It worked. Ellie was distracted, she was smiling, and she didn't look as if she would cry anymore.

Mademoiselle Francesca restuffed her pockets full of fairy dust and appeared back at the forest with Broderick by her side. Broderick brought a picnic basket chockablock full of fairy treats and goodies. Boris's eyes darted toward the basket, his mouth watering. Noticing the girls playing on the back of Ellie's hand, Mademoiselle Francesca almost fainted.

"*Girls!*" Mademoiselle shrieked so loudly that Ellie stopped laughing, and Lilly froze.

"We're watching them closely," Monsieur Pierre assured her. He continued in a whisper, "Agent Chester is by Lilly's side, and Agent Arley is between Pearle and Rosie. We were desperate. The child is sad, mad, and hungry."

"Forgive me, Monsieur, but that still doesn't put my mind at ease. The child is still so large compared to the fairlings."

"See, I said the same thing!" Boris whispered to Jack.

"It was that or Ellie was going to wander farther into the forest to look for her parents and food."

"If I may," Broderick interjected. "I think it's time she eats something, and our fairlings as well." Worried, Broderick looked at the basket. "Although I'm not sure there's enough food for everyone, given the size of the child."

"It might be the first time Boris won't complain about his tummy rumbling." Jack laughed. "But I won't complain, either; let the giant eat first, so she doesn't eat us."

Broderick handed Lilly a fairy watercress sandwich for Ellie. Ellie stared at the tiny sandwich that Lilly held in her hand. She had never seen a sandwich so small in all her life.

"Broderick makes the best sandwiches," Lilly gushed.

"Who's Broderick?"

Lilly pointed to Broderick, who instinctively waved all eight hands at once. Ellie smiled. How funny to see a spider wearing a sweater! She ate all the watercress sandwiches that Broderick had prepared. They were delicious, and Ellie usually didn't like anything green her mommy prepared for her. Next, Rosie handed her a fairy delight; it melted in her mouth.

"Ohhhhh, that's good. Can I have another one of those?"

"Please," Lilly instinctively answered. Embarrassed she'd corrected the child, she handed

Ellie another fairy treat. "You most certainly may have another one or two if you like."

"She can't help herself," Jack chuckled. "Lilly, always bossy, correcting everyone."

Ellie washed down her meal with sweet elderberry tea. She'd never had elderberry tea before, but her tastebuds quite enjoyed the flavor. Just as Boris feared, Ellie ate everything Broderick had prepared for those participating in the moss bomb war that day. It was impossible to hide his disappointment, especially as his hunger pangs grew stronger. Monsieur Pierre comforted Boris by telling him Cook would rustle up a batch of fairy stew and dumplings, his favorite, as soon as Ellie was reunited with her family. Disappointed, hungry, and tired, Boris challenged Jack to a guessing game as they waited to see what they were supposed to do next.

The search party looking for the child had been spotted closer than ever; they needed to reunite Ellie with her family sooner rather than later. The time was upon them; they had to move the child eastward.

"Darkness will be upon us soon; we'll move then!" Agent Arley instructed. "When it's time to make our move, we'll ask Lilly to assist. Ellie seems to like her."

Mademoiselle Francesca watched Lilly, who was now standing on Ellie's knee, Chester by her side. Though in much closer proximity than she would have liked, Lilly did help the child, and if necessary, Lilly had the perfect escape route: shoot upward, escaping danger. Pearle and Rosie hovered close by to help entertain Ellie and watch over Lilly. Boris and Jack, leaning on a tree trunk, listened as Lilly told Ellie another story. Lilly had a knack for telling the best stories. She'd told Boris several stories when he'd crashed through the trees, hurt his ankle, and they were both stuck in the woods. Even Jack liked to listen to Lilly's stories. One more story and they'd nod off; a little rest was good for everyone, especially since they were about to head out into the dark forest!

Chapter 14
Follow the Fairy

Fireflies dancing in the sky assured Agent Arley it was time to make a move. Nightfall had blanketed the forest with a sheet of darkness, providing the extra layer of protection they'd need as they traveled. Mademoiselle Francesca joined Chester by Lilly's side as she danced on top of Ellie's hand. Ellie laughed out loud as Lilly's toes brushed her skin and tickled her. Chester smiled at the child; she had such a lovely face, and despite her size didn't seem threatening at all. Ellie couldn't see Chester, but Mademoiselle Francesca was quite visible, and Ellie felt comforted by Mademoiselle's soft voice when she spoke to her.

"Ellie, a little birdie told me your favorite fairy treat was Broderick's famous fairy delights. Is that true, dear?"

Ellie smiled and nodded her head. "Yes, they were the bestest thing I've ever tasted, ever." She giggled. "I'd like to eat those again."

"I believe others have stated that very same thing." Hovering up, up, and up until she was face-to-face with Ellie, Mademoiselle knew it was time to prepare their gigantic stranger to travel through the night. "I'm certain if you're brave on our next adventure, Broderick will make some more fairy treats for you."

A sweet smile crossed Mademoiselle's face as she spoke to their little intruder, knowing it was important she didn't scare or alarm her as they prepared to move. Mademoiselle chose her words very carefully. The forest could be a scary place, especially at night, and though the child was huge to them, Mademoiselle was well aware of the dangers the forest held for anyone, particularly a child.

"Ellie, dear, your mommy is worried about you because she can't find you."

Ellie stopped smiling as images of her mommy popped into her head. Now sad, she hung onto every word Mademoiselle said. Her soft voice and kind eyes helped comfort her, and Ellie managed to fight back her tears despite the sadness she once again felt.

"Don't worry. We're going to take you to a place where your mommy will find you, but you must listen closely and do exactly what we ask you to do." Mademoiselle stared into Ellie's big brown eyes. "Do you understand?"

Ellie nodded; thinking of seeing her mommy and daddy again made her happy. Mademoiselle, hovering in one spot for too long, adjusted her wings.

"May I," Mademoiselle asked, pointing to Ellie's hand, "sit with you and Lilly?"

Ellie held out her hand, and Mademoiselle Francesca landed lightly next to Lilly. Boris didn't dare look. Mademoiselle, just like Lilly, could be a squashed fairy at any given moment. What on earth would the colony do if they lost Mademoiselle and Lilly?! Grateful Monsieur had not asked him to play with the giant child, Boris was still determined to try to help. Raising his hand, he wondered if there was anything he and Jack could do to help. Desperately he hoped that there wasn't, but at least he volunteered. Knowing Boris was terrified, and Jack wasn't too keen either, Monsieur Pierre was proud the two young fairlings offered at all. Ruffling the top of Boris's hair, Monsieur suggested the boys bring up the rear with Monsieur Claude when it was time to leave. Relieved they didn't have to be anywhere near the human child and excited they could fly in the back with Monsieur Claude, Boris and Jack quickly agreed before Monsieur Pierre changed his mind.

Mademoiselle Francesca instructed Lilly to stay close by her side and, when instructed, fly in front of

Ellie when it was time to depart. Lilly proudly agreed. Mademoiselle instructed Ellie to keep her eyes on Lilly as they traveled, and her ears open. Ellie understood what Mademoiselle Francesca had asked her to do: follow and listen despite her heavy heart. Broderick lowered himself from the branch above and landed on top of Ellie's knee. He walked around in circles and tickled her kneecap with one of his legs. Ellie couldn't figure out which leg he'd used, and Lilly couldn't stop giggling.

"I've never seen a spider that wears clothes, can cook, talks, and plays," Ellie hollered. "Can Broderick come home with me?"

Broderick stopped moving and sat down next to Lilly. "What a lovely thought, dear," he replied. "But how would I repair all of these webs if I'm in the city?" He pointed upwards into the branches and, for the first time, Ellie noticed several beautiful webs strung out across them.

Broderick pointed to Lilly. "And if I leave Lilly, who will knit her scarves and mittens for the winter?"

He put one of his arms around Lilly and hugged her gently.

"Lilly, would you miss me if I were gone?"

"Miss you?" Lilly cried. "Broderick, I think my heart would break." Playfully wagging a finger at Broderick, she asked, "Why would you ask such a silly thing?"

Broderick didn't answer, but Ellie did. "OK, funny little spider. I won't take you with me. But you must promise to play with me the next time I visit."

"If there's a next time, I promise to prepare your favorite fairy treat and play with you."

"It's time to head out," Agent Arley announced. "Does the child know what to do?"

Mademoiselle glanced at Ellie. "Ellie, are you ready?"

Ellie nodded her head. "Yes, ma'am."

"She's as ready as she's ever going to be," Mademoiselle responded as she instructed the fairies to prepare to fly. "Fairlings, please take your positions."

"Ellie, remember to keep your eyes on me," Lilly whispered. "If your eyes get tired, or you can't see me, follow your feet. Mademoiselle will hold your hand."

Ellie nodded. "I remember what Mademoiselle said. Follow Lilly, that's you." She pointed to Lilly. "Mademoiselle also said to look at my feet if I can't see you, and the trail would sparkle and light up. Like magic!"

Lilly grinned. "That's right, Ellie. Fairy dust: it *is* kinda like magic. It's amazing, just like you. Now, are you ready for our adventure?"

Saying goodbye to Broderick made Ellie sad, but the thought of finding her mommy and daddy made her feel happy inside. The air was starting to chill, and the night sky was dimming. It would be completely dark soon, and Ellie knew she feared the dark.

"Time for our game, Ellie—follow the fairy; that's me."

Lilly smiled with pride. The agents would lead, but Lilly had the responsibility of guiding Ellie through the forest. Mademoiselle asked Lilly to count.

"On the count of three then, Lilly, if you please, three, not four."

Lilly began to count. "One a fairy, two a fairy, three a fairy."

With the wave of her hand, Mademoiselle Francesca suddenly doused Lilly in so much fairy dust she looked like a bright beacon shining in the forest. Ellie couldn't contain her excitement and cried out with such joy that Agent Arley wondered if she'd ever settle down. Madame Louise flew to Lilly's side and whispered words of support and encouragement.

"The agents and Liam will lead, you will be next, and of course, Ellie will follow you. You are amazing!"

"What about Boris and Jack?"

"Monsieur Claude is with them and some of the agents bringing up the rear with the rest of our group."

Chester flew beside Lilly. Ellie couldn't see him, but Lilly felt better knowing he was right there by her side. He motioned to his ear, and Lilly knew that meant she was to keep her ears open. As the night sky darkened, Ellie started to get scared, but Mademoiselle Francesca, in her sweetest voice, assured her all was well.

"Keep your eyes on Lilly, dear, and don't worry about the night owl singing; he means no harm and certainly doesn't mean to scare you. He's singing for you; isn't that lovely?"

Ellie wasn't sure if she liked the owl's song, but she did feel better about the strange noises she was hearing. Putting one foot in front of the other, Ellie forged ahead as Lilly, the tiny beacon of light, stayed in front of her. Lilly continued to sing at the top of her lungs. Gingerly they made their way through the thicket and onto the forest path. Ellie didn't know which was more entertaining: Lilly, or that every footstep she took lit up, sparkly and bright. As instructed by Mademoiselle, the path was laced with fairy dust just in case Ellie lost sight of Lilly in the dark.

"Follow the fairy, Ellie, follow me," Lilly sang. *"Follow the fairy, Ellie, one step at a time. Follow the fairy, Ellie, and you'll be fine."*

What if they couldn't deliver the child unseen? Their fate could be too terrible to imagine. Boris shuddered at the thought of the unknown and kept going.

"Something wrong, mate?" Jack quizzed, noticing Boris had an odd look on his face.

Boris nodded. "What if the human's parents find us first?"

"I never thought about that; that could be tragic!"

Jack tried to put his friend's mind at ease. "The elders must have a plan in place, Boris, and we're an active part of it. They wouldn't put our colony at risk."

Boris dodged branch after branch as they followed Lilly through the forest. Monsieur Pierre appeared next to the boys.

"We're going to leave Ellie directly in the path of the human search party and watch her from the underbrush to ensure she's safe. Be prepared to stop when the signal is given."

"See, the elders do have a plan; we're in good hands," Jack smirked.

Fatigue started to set in, and despite how hard Lilly tried, her wings slowed down. Dodging branches in the dark after a full day of play was taking its toll. Chester gently encouraged her to push ahead and keep her wings engaged despite her fatigue and hunger. She was a star! Nonstop singing and keeping Ellie's mind off the long walk in the dark. Ellie's hands constantly reached toward Lilly in fun, trying to capture the beautiful fairy in her chubby little hands. Ellie had no idea that it took every ounce of strength Lilly had left to zigzag out of her reach. Ellie's giggle was contagious; she laughed the whole time that she followed Lilly through the trees. Each time Lilly slipped through Ellie's fingers, Ellie tried to catch her again; she was enjoying this game of *following the fairy*. Relieved the child's mind was occupied by Lilly, the elders forged ahead, grateful for their gifted fairling's desire and ability to help. Agents had been dispatched to locate the human search party and report back. Mademoiselle Francesca was convinced they would hear word soon about where to leave Ellie.

"You're doing great, little one," Chester whispered. "Ellie has yet to look down at the glittery path; she's having too much fun chasing you."

Chester's kind words and comforting smile were all the encouragement Lilly needed. Flying as fast as she could in and out of Ellie's hands, singing at the top of her lungs, she continued to lead the way. Suddenly the group came to a screeching halt! A scout had spotted the humans; Ellie's parents were in sight!

Chapter 15
Seek the Seekers

Agent Arley, unlike many agents who were visible to only a few, had the luxury of being in everyone's presence at will. Volunteering to be in the front of the line to lead the fairies through the forest, he suddenly came to an abrupt stop. A raised hand signaled everyone to follow his lead and disengage their wings. Hovering in place, they all waited to see what they should do next. Pointing away from the path, Agent Arley darted toward the foliage; the fairlings and the elders followed and took cover. Ellie, realizing she was suddenly alone in the dark, felt afraid. Her mouth turned down into a frown, and her big brown eyes welled up with water. One blink and Agent Arley knew the tears would spill over her eyelids and pour down her cheeks. Jack could see the desperation in Agent Arley's face, and he tried to intervene. Tugging at Monsieur Pierre's arm, Jack whispered in Monsieur's ear.

"Sir, Ellie is about to cry. I don't think Lilly should have left her side." He pointed to Ellie. "What should we do?"

Worried, Monsieur replied, "Where is Lilly?"

Mademoiselle Francesca appeared beside Monsieur Pierre, opened her mouth to speak, but didn't get a chance to say a word. Monsieur Pierre pointed to Ellie.

"Oh, no! She's doing it; she's going to blow!"

Ellie's tears were flowing uncontrollably, and the sound she made was heartbreaking and loud. Sad, tired, hungry, cold, and now scared, Ellie couldn't hold her tears back any longer. Without hesitation, Mademoiselle Francesca snapped her fingers, and an exhausted Lilly, though Mademoiselle had no idea how, appeared at her side. Holding her hand in hers, Mademoiselle and Lilly disappeared, only to reappear in front of a sobbing Ellie. Everyone held their breaths as each tear Ellie shed splashed and drenched Mademoiselle and Lilly to the bone. Sprinkling fairy dust all over the top of their heads, Mademoiselle created the most beautiful canopy protecting them from Ellie's gigantic tears. Ellie's howls turned into quieter sobs once she realized Lilly and Mademoiselle had once again joined her. As Ellie's sobs grew farther and farther apart, Mademoiselle Francesca finally spoke.

"Now, now, dear, we're so close to reuniting you with your parents." Handing Ellie a handkerchief, she continued speaking. "Just a little while longer, that's all, and you'll be reunited with your family."

Ellie took the tiny handkerchief but wiped her face with the sleeve of her shirt. Opening the palm of her hand, she waited for Lilly to climb on. Lilly was exhausted and stepped onto Ellie's hand without thinking and flopped down in a pile in the middle of Ellie's hand. Chester reached for Lilly's arm, but as she sat down, she escaped his grasp. Mademoiselle Francesca, Chester, and everyone watching from a clump of brush gasped. Chester didn't like Lilly taking such risks, especially when the tiny fairling was so tired. Ellie's palm was facing upwards, not down. How could Lilly get up and fly, moving out of the way in time, if the child accidentally closed her hand? A squashed fairy, especially a gifted one, wasn't going to happen on his watch! Even though Ellie couldn't see him, Chester placed himself right next to Lilly on the palm of Ellie's hand. Mademoiselle had never been so relieved that Chester was by Lilly's side. Lilly, too tired to think, was confused. What was all the fuss about anyway? Knowing Lilly was with her again, Ellie stopped crying and watched the beautiful sparkling fairy sitting in her hand as if she was the most precious thing she'd ever seen. Chester continued to stand guard.

"Lilly will stay with you for a while longer," Mademoiselle whispered.

Ellie nodded. Mademoiselle tried to diffuse the dangerous situation Lilly unknowingly found herself in. As Mademoiselle flew toward Lilly, Ellie started to close her fingers around the fairy; Mademoiselle backed off. Chester looked worried as he stood over an exhausted little fairy.

"Ellie, Lilly is so tired, just like you. I'm afraid she may fall asleep in your hand, and you may fall asleep and drop her." Mademoiselle didn't dare say squash her. She stood on Ellie's arm. "We're about to walk again, just a little way, and it would be best if Lilly sat on your shoulder for the rest of the journey. Is that OK with you?"

Ellie thought about it for a moment. She was tired and didn't want to walk anymore, but finally, she agreed to let Lilly move. Lilly positioned herself on Ellie's shoulder, and thankfully Boris and Jack volunteered to sit with her. Chester was still by Lilly's side, relieved she was out of the child's clutches. Agent Arley gave the signal, and everyone fell back into position and moved once again for the last time through the forest.

"Seekers seeking the child are just ahead," Agent Micha informed Agent Arley. "Are you prepared to end the mission here?"

Agent Arley, Agent Micha, and Mademoiselle Francesca discussed the spot on the path where they would leave Ellie after they safely retrieved Lilly. Mademoiselle Francesca spoke up. "We can't leave Ellie alone; we'll have to watch over her until she's in the arms of her parents. It's our duty."

Agent Langston suddenly appeared out of nowhere and stood between them.

"Mademoiselle, of course, is right. Despite how we feel about this dangerous mission, we must not abandon the child; the woods are too dangerous. We'll wait with the child until she has been reunited with the humans. She's right; it is our duty."

They'd walk a little farther to an opening on the path, a perfect spot where Ellie was sure to be seen by the human search party. Carefully they'd retrieve their sweet Lilly, and make sure everyone was under cover and safe while they waited for the reunion of Ellie and her parents to take place.

Chapter 16
That's My Mommy!

Struggling to keep her eyes open, Lilly forced herself to chat with Ellie and keep her engaged in conversation. Lilly's voice distracted Ellie as she trudged along the path to the opening in the forest where she unknowingly would be left. Agents staked out treetops, ready to signal when Ellie's parents and the search party were in sight. Lilly noticed how anxious Mademoiselle seemed, and knew it was almost time to reunite Ellie and her parents. Dreading the unavoidable proximity to the humans they were about to encounter, Boris felt sick to his stomach. Green. He turned green, and he hadn't even been playing Spin a Fairling Green.

Agent Langston and Agent Micha were seated high in the branches of a tall oak tree. Each time a twig snapped, or leaves crunched, their ears perked up. No need to track the humans anymore; they were headed straight toward them. It was only a matter of minutes before they'd be in sight. An owl hooted and scattered leaves into the night sky as it flew away. Something or someone had startled it. Ellie stopped talking to Lilly and listened. The agents had to retrieve Lilly now!

Voices could be heard in the distance—human voices were bouncing off the trees as they came closer and closer toward them. The search party seeking the child was about to run into the elders who had escorted her and had left her to be found. Quick as lightening, the agents warned the elders; the time had come. The elders hid the fairlings under the brush and foliage as quickly as they could. Once hidden, they dodged out of sight themselves. Lilly moved once more to the palm of Ellie's hand, surrounded by Chester, Mademoiselle Francesca, and Agent Arley.

"Lilly, be ready to fly, but do not fear if we remove you first," Chester whispered in Lilly's ear. "Just be ready."

Lilly, trembling from exhaustion, tried to engage her wings, but they barely moved. Fear and anxiety were written all over her face, but Mademoiselle put her mind at ease before she panicked.

"We'll carry you, dear. Do not worry; we will not leave you here."

"*Ellie, Ellie, Elllllllllie.*"

Voices cried out repeatedly. Indescribable pain attached to the voices radiated through the vast darkness. Over and over, they called out Ellie's name.

"*Ellie. Ellie, where are you?*"

Ellie was about to be found by her humans right where they had so carefully placed her; Lilly was still in the palm of Ellie's hand.

"What about Lilly?" Boris asked with such terror in his voice even Jack couldn't comfort him.

Grateful the unexpected adventure was almost over, Mademoiselle Francesca's eyes darted toward sleepy little Lilly. What a trooper she had been. Innocently unaware of the danger Ellie posed to her, she had unselfishly comforted the child, and now as she sat in the palm of the Ellie's hand, they could not fail her! Mademoiselle, fearing an exhausted Ellie might accidentally squeeze a sleepy fairy too tight, focused on a plan to retrieve her sweet little fairy, Lilly.

The mere mention of leaving Ellie alone on the trail caused Ellie to cry hysterically; that was it! Mademoiselle wanted Ellie to cry as hard as she possibly could; her parents were close enough to hear her. Hovering at eye level with Ellie, Mademoiselle explained that it was time for Lilly to retreat to the trees. She landed on Ellie's hand and grasped Lilly's hand in hers. A voice from the search party caught Ellie's attention, one she recognized.

"Be ready," Chester whispered. "We're about to get you out of here."

Ellie suddenly jumped to her feet.

"Mommy? That's my mommy!"

Excited to hear her mommy's voice, Mademoiselle Francesca knew it was now or never to save Lilly. She shot up into the sky, Lilly's hand still in hers, ready to dart toward the brush. To her horror, Lilly's hand slipped out of her grasp, and no matter how hard Chester tried, he couldn't catch Lilly as she tumbled back into Ellie's hand. Boris, peeking out from under a leaf, covered his own mouth for fear of screaming. Mademoiselle, shocked, almost froze but kept her wits about her as Ellie called out to her mommy.

"Mommy! Mommy! Look! I have a fairy."

Mademoiselle Francesca whispered Ellie's name in her ear.

"Ellie."

"That's my mommy. Did you hear her?"

"I did," answered Mademoiselle. "Wonderful news; it's time to go home, and I'm going to douse you in fairy dust, just like Lilly, so you'll light up in the dark and your mommy will find you."

Ellie grinned. She'd never been covered from head to toe in fairy dust before! Holding out both of her arms, she waited for Mademoiselle to douse her in fairy dust. Ellie closed her eyes. What if the dust got in her eyes; would it hurt? She waited; nothing happened. Ellie opened one eye.

"I'm not glowing."

She squeezed her eyes shut and waited. Did she feel any different? No. Why wasn't she glowing? Puzzled, she asked Mademoiselle why she wasn't glowing.

Mademoiselle Francesca flew to Ellie's hand and tapped her fingers.

"I can't dust you with Lilly in your hand; it won't work."

"Why?" Ellie whined.

"Why what, dear?"

"Why won't the glow work with Lilly in my hand?"

Mademoiselle Francesca stayed as calm as she possibly could despite the horrendous situation. Ellie's parents, the humans, were only a few feet away and running toward them.

"Ellie, it's dark, and once your mommy turns that corner, she won't see you unless you're glowing."

"That's my mommy!" she squealed. "Mommy! Mommy, over here!"

Mademoiselle pointed to Ellie's hand and whispered, "Lilly is still in your hand."

Ellie slowly opened up her hand. Lilly lay in a crumpled pile in the palm of Ellie's hand, Mademoiselle Francesca's heart almost stopped, until Lilly raised her sleepy head.

"I can't dust you while Lilly is in your hand, because fairies are dust-blockers."

Lilly gave Mademoiselle the strangest look but didn't say a word. She'd never heard of such a thing, but if Mademoiselle said fairies could block dust, then fairies blocked dust!

Ellie shook her head and clamped her fingers around Lilly again, refusing to turn over her new best friend. Boris and Jack nervously looked on. Boris's voice was squeaky at best, but he asked Jack why Ellie hadn't let Lilly go yet.

"I don't know, Boris, but I'm sure she will let her go any minute. Look, Mademoiselle Francesca is talking with Ellie right now."

Mademoiselle Francesca wriggled her nose and gently tapped the end of Ellie's nose.

"Humans require a lot more dust than we generally use, and too much dust tickles our noses. It's tickling mine right now, and if that's not bad enough, it makes our eyes water. Lilly won't be able to help herself. She'll blow away all the extra dust sprinkled on you, blocking your glow because it will tickle her nose."

"Like allergies?" Ellie asked.

"Yes, like allergies." Mademoiselle looked Ellie in the eye and firmly demanded she let go of Lilly. "Ellie, let go of Lilly now!"

Ellie wanted to keep Lilly. Her mommy had never met a fairy before, and how lovely it would be to introduce her to her new friend. But as soon as Ellie spotted her mommy, she unclenched the palm of her hand without even realizing it. Mademoiselle Francesca flew in as if her life depended on it, scooped Lilly up, handed her to Chester, doused Ellie with the fairy dust she had left, and disappeared. Ellie, glowing from head to toe, rushed toward her mommy. A gigantic human darted toward the glowing child, still calling her name, but the tone was different.

"*Ellie. Ellie!*"

"It's me, Mommy."

Ellie's mommy fell on her knees as she grabbed her, hugged her, and kissed her all over her face. Holding her close and crying happy tears, she hadn't even asked why her child was a beacon in the forest.

"She must be starving and thirsty," her daddy yelled. "Where are the crackers and the water?"

"I'm not hungry, Daddy," Ellie replied. "I ate Broderick's fairy watercress sandwiches, and he made some fairy delights, which were my very favorite." She hesitated. "And I drank fairy elderberry tea."

"Broderick?" Ellie's parents asked with concern in their voices. "Who's Broderick?"

"Broderick. Broderick, he's a funny spider. He cooks and wears sweaters." Ellie giggled. "He's my friend, and so is Lilly."

Puzzled, her parents quizzed her. "Who's Lilly?"

"Broderick is a spider who cooks and knits. Lilly is a fairy, and so are the others, Mademoiselle Francesca and Madame Louise." Ellie looked around her for the fairies. "Boris, he's funny, and Jack is very nice but doesn't talk much; they took care of me and brought me here."

Wrapping Ellie in a blanket, they scooped her up and held her close. Concerned, they chatted among themselves.

"She's clearly dehydrated and delusional," Ellie's daddy whispered under his breath. "We need to get her to the hospital immediately for an evaluation."

Ellie kept trying to explain, but no one seemed to understand.

"Mademoiselle Francesca covered me in fairy dust, see? I'm glowing from head to toe. That's so you could find me in the dark." Ellie lowered her voice. "It's so dark and scary, and I was afraid."

Ellie's Mommy held her close to her chest. Odd, she was glowing from head to toe in something, but what? They didn't know. Turning to leave, Ellie suddenly yelled and pointed to the thicket. Chester's heart stopped as he watched Ellie try to direct her parents to where they had hidden all the fairlings.

"Can we please say goodbye to Lilly and the others?" she asked. "They're over there, in those bushes."

Hesitantly, her mommy answered. "I think we should say goodbye from here, don't you? It's very late, and I'm sure they're sleeping by now, just like you should be."

Ellie wasn't convinced they were all asleep, but she was too tired to argue. Maybe she could come back and visit Lilly and the others someday.

"Bye, Lilly. See you soon!"

"Oh, my fairy goodness!" Boris whispered to Jack. "I hope we never see them again; did you see the size of those grown humans?"

It was no wonder the elders were continually worried about humans in the forest. Jack, too stunned to speak, managed to nudge Boris as they stared in horror at the sheer size of the humans now holding Ellie in their arms. Ellie didn't seem afraid, but the size of the humans surrounding her were enough to terrify the fairlings, the elders, and the agents!

Chapter 17
Back to the Colony

Between Boris's teeth chattering, Lilly's body trembling, and Jack pulling his shirt collar up around his neck, Mademoiselle knew the chill in the night air was too much for the exhausted fairies to handle. The possibility of their wings locking up due to the loss of body heat was highly likely if they didn't move fast. Spending the night in the forest was simply out of the question! Besides wing lock, they couldn't see a thing, strange noises of who-knew-what animal was lurking in the background, and all of them needed food. Monsieur Pierre appeared at Mademoiselle Francesca's side; he looked worried.

"We can't stay here, but I know you already agree." Hesitating, he added, "Any ideas?"

"I'm worried the fairlings are too weak to fly back, not to mention they'd get wing lock anyway because of the cold. I'm out of dust, but it's imperative we leave the forest. Danger lurks, and we can't risk staying here any longer."

Chester appeared between Mademoiselle Francesca and Monsieur Pierre. He winked and nodded at Lilly, a little assurance that they had a plan or at least giving the impression that they were working on one. A glance at the sleepy fairlings gathered around Madame Louise, and he knew they had no choice but to act fast. A blast of cool air blew down the back of Monsieur Pierre's neck, causing him to shudder. The wind was blowing stronger, sounded eerie, and howled and whipped through the trees, snapping branches as if it were easy.

"I have a plan, so please don't worry. Agent Arley and the others are going to assist." Chester pointed up into branches of the trees. "They're discussing my plan now."

Chester knew it would be impossible to transport the fairlings back as a group; exhausted, they would never make it out of the forest. Each fairling would have to be transported or towed by an elder or an agent in pairs. The elders and agents would use their energy and strength to pull the fairlings' little bodies alongside of them and fly them back to the colony.

"This way, they will not have to fly and exert any energy, except to hold hands, which shouldn't be an issue."

"If only I weren't out of fairy dust," Mademoiselle sighed, "I could have sprinkled them all, and we could have transported them all at the same time."

"We can't worry about what we can't change, Mademoiselle. You used the dust wisely, and Ellie is safe. We must focus on the task at hand and how we can manage it."

"Agreed, Chester. Once the first group arrives at the colony, they can send back the fairy dust."

"Agree. If the dust monitor cannot be reached to dole out the dust, we'll bring back every available elder to help fly the young ones back." He disappeared, only to reappear again. "I'll also notify Cook to start a batch of fairy stew and ask the bath monitor to run hot baths. Food before baths today."

Everyone agreed. Boris was sick to his stomach since he hadn't eaten a bite since breakfast, not even a snack. Mademoiselle thanked her friend, Chester, and worked with Monsieur Pierre to organize the fairies and get them home. Madame Louise gently woke up those that had fallen asleep. Lilly stirred, tried to open her eyes but was so exhausted from keeping Ellie entertained, she could barely stand up. No fairy had flown as long or as hard as she had. Keeping her eyes open was nearly impossible, and the thought of even trying to engage her wings one more time was overwhelming. Chester scooped her up and placed her in Mademoiselle Francesca's arms.

"Will you please carry her, and I will follow you with two others?"

Mademoiselle Francesca's heart sank as she realized it might take Lilly several days to recover. Cradling her in her arms, she kissed the top of Lilly's head. Lilly didn't even know she was in Mademoiselle's arms. She barely stirred.

"Of course I will. After all, Lilly saved the day, really, didn't she?"

Chester would escort two fairlings back to the colony, as would Madame Louise and each agent still in the forest. Monsieur Pierre and Monsieur Claude would wait in the forest with the rest of the young ones until the others returned for the next group of fairlings. Hoping the dust monitor was still awake and would dole out extra dust, Chester flew with his fingers crossed. Madame Louise held Rosie and Ivy's hands tightly in hers. Too tired to keep up, she would pull them alongside her. An invisible agent grabbed

Boris by the arm and pulled him to his feet. Unable to see who it was scared Boris to death, and he thought the forest was attacking him.

"Ahhhhhhhh!"

Monsieur Pierre appeared in front of him and ruffled Boris's mop of dark brown hair.

"It's all right, Boris, you can always trust the agents. You can't see them, but they can see you, and they're always present to protect you."

Boris still wasn't sure but agreed to go with the agents because he did trust Monsieur Pierre, who had assured him he was in good hands. As exhausted as Jack was, it didn't stop him from laughing at his friend's distress, Boris's scream. Jack reached over to shove Boris, but before Jack could lay a hand on him, out of thin air, an agent grabbed his arm and tapped the top of his hand, scaring *Jack* half to death.

"Now, now, Jack, be nice," a voice seemingly belonging to no one firmly instructed.

Jack froze, buttoned up his lip, and decided it was best if he didn't say another word! Whoever was standing next to him had a firm grip on his arm, and by the looks of Boris, had a firm grip on him as well. Without warning, the two boys were hovering several inches off the ground. Several! They had only ever been cleared for two inches, not three, not four, and certainly not more by their flight instructor. Jack and Boris exchanged looks, but before they could say anything, a loud voice interrupted them.

"Prepare to fly," the voice commanded. "Spread your wings but do not engage. I repeat, do not engage! You will not be flying this evening but pulled back to the colony by your escort."

Grateful, the boys did as they were told; neither one thought they could possibly fly anymore anyway. Suddenly they shot into the air; all the fairlings and elders were below. Additional instructions were given, and for a second, it felt as if they were about to go on another adventure until they heard the scary words of the invisible commander speaking.

"Trust me, it will be impossible for you to keep up; therefore, please don't try. If you do engage your wings, they will bend and possibly snap! Broken wings take a lonnnnng time to heal. You don't want a broken wing, do you?"

Boris trembled at the thought and immediately shook his head; he didn't want a broken anything. Jack wasn't too happy about the possibility of breaking a wing either but didn't understand how they'd fly back to the colony without engaging their wings. There was no way he was going to ask; buckle up and go with the flow, he told himself.

"Hold my hand as tightly as you can, and I will fly for all of us. Try not to let go. I'll pull you alongside me as I fly, but we'll be going faster than you're used to flying. If you hold on to me, and I hold on to you, we should be just fine."

Without warning, the boys suddenly shot off. They'd never flown at such heights or such speed before, and Jack absolutely loved it! If he could only be cleared to fly at such altitudes and such speeds, the exploring he could do! The wind whipped through their hair and over their faces. Jack could barely open his eyes to see where they were going but forced them open, hoping not to miss the thrill ride. Boris had one eye open, and his free hand held his queasy tummy. Was it possible for a fairy to be afraid of heights? Boris was scared to death and didn't dare look down. The other agents soon caught up with them, fairlings alongside, and Mademoiselle Francesca flew past them cradling little Lilly in her arms. Madame Louise trailed behind, escorting Rosie and Ivy. They arrived at the colony in record time. Tired, cold, and hungry!

Elders greeted the groups as they arrived with warm blankets and ushered them into the dining hall. The delicious smell of fairy stew wafted toward them, and it smelled so good they could almost taste it before they took a bite. Freshly baked bread sat on every table, and hot rosehip tea had already been poured. As Cook served the stew, the elders and agents set off to escort back the last group of exhausted fairlings with fairy dust in hand to speed up their journey.

Lilly took a sip of the hot rosehip tea. As it trickled down her throat, the liquid warmed her entire body. Dipping her bread into the fairy stew, Lilly took bite after bite, eating much faster than she usually did. Surprising even herself, she ate all of it. Boris was already on his second serving, and Cook couldn't help but smile as she filled up his bowl. It pleased her to see him eat so well, especially after a night like they'd just experienced. He must have been famished. Spoons clattered in bowls, teacups clanged on saucers, but other than that, not a sound could be heard in the dining hall as the fairlings ate their supper. Jack helped place chocolate chip fairy bites on every table, but Lilly was too stuffed and too tired to eat another bite. Without saying a word, she pushed hers over to Boris. Boris, grateful for the extra fairy bites, thanked her, and shoved them in his mouth.

"Bathing rooms," Madame Francesca instructed. "And then straight off to bed. There'll be plenty of time to chitchat about your adventure tomorrow."

Not one fairy complained! Feet shuffled down the hallway, and barely a whisper could be heard. Bath. Bed. What a treat after such an ordeal!

Chapter 18
Unbelievable

Sunshine poured through the windows; the warmth of the sun tingled the sleeping fairies' cheeks as they slept. Madame Louise tiptoed past each bed and smiled. Pearle woke up first. Noticing her friends were still fast asleep, she wondered if she should still lay there, but she felt rested. Madame Louise appeared at the side of her bed and playfully scooped her up, only to disappear and reappear in the bathing room. Pearle couldn't help but giggle. Madame Louise never did that; how fun!

"Madame Louise, is there something wrong with my chariot?"

"No, sweet Pearle, your chariot is fine. In fact, I'm about to go and fetch it for you. However, did you by chance notice your friends are still sleeping?"

Pearle nodded; she had noticed the others still fast asleep. Rosie was usually the first one up, and she *was* still sound asleep in her bed. Ivy was often second, and Lilly, well, Pearle usually had to wake Lilly up. But exhaustion from the excitement the day before had gotten the best of them. Being whisked away to the bathing room by Madame Louise only added to the excitement that Pearle still felt.

"I wondered if I should go back to sleep," Pearle responded. "But I wasn't tired."

Madame tapped her gently on the nose. "As if you could," she said with a grin. "I've yet to see you go back to sleep even when you are tired. You fight sleep, little one." Madame Louise headed toward the door, but not before giving Pearle specific instructions.

"Wash your face, clean your teeth, brush your hair, and straighten your wings. As soon as Madame Charlotte takes her post as dorm monitor, I'll return with a clean dress and your chariot, and then we'll eat breakfast together."

Pearle's smile was as wide as her face. How lovely to eat breakfast with Madame Louise; they had so much to talk about this morning. Quickly, Pearle set about straightening her wings. The clattering sound bouncing down the hall alerted her that Madame Louise was nearby with her chariot in tow. The thought of cleaning dirty, smelly mud and swampy moss off her chariot was confirmation that she'd done the right thing by flying the entire way without her chariot. It would have been impossible to push the chariot through the woods, and though her wings were now weak and tired, she wouldn't have missed the adventure for all the fairy twists in the world. Madame Louise hugged her close before gently placing her safely in the chariot. How proud they were of her for keeping up as she had, resting only when the others did, and perching on the branches with her legs dangling to ensure she could take off when they were all on the move again. What was supposed to have been a few hours of fairy fun had turned into something quite different, an adventure with twists and turns that no one could have expected.

"Let's chat while we eat; I'm starving, aren't you?"

The smell of fresh fairy crumpets hit them as soon as they opened the dining hall door. The place was buzzing, as usual. Fairies were making their breakfast selections, others putting their trays away, and chatter radiated throughout the dining hall as if nothing unusual had happened at all. Was it possible those that hadn't joined them had no idea what had happened? Pearle's eyes scanned the tables. Where she usually sat with her friends was empty. Madame Louise, carrying two trays, motioned for Pearle to join her at a table close to the boys, who were already on their second serving of porridge and hot iced buns.

Boris had just put his spoon in his mouth when Jack slapped him on the back. The porridge flew from Boris's mouth all over the table. Laughing, Boris snuck a slimy moss bomb from his pocket and shoved it in the bowl of porridge that Jack had just set down on the table. Jack took one bite, realized Boris had pulled a fast one, and both boys burst out laughing. Boris slid a fairy crumpet toward Jack as a peace offering; though Jack had started that round, Boris had indeed won it.

"Well, Madame, what do you think about our adventure from yesterday?" Pearle asked before taking a big bite of fairy crumpet with jelly and butter..

Madame Louise set her teacup in her saucer, took a deep breath, and lowered her voice so she wouldn't alarm anyone.

"You're not going to believe this, Pearle, but I think running smack into the human child was both scary and exhilarating."

"I understand," Pearle replied sheepishly. "I hate to admit it, though Ellie seemed like a very nice human, I was frozen in fear most of the time. In fact, at one point, I had to force my wings to engage when it was time to fly because they were frozen stiff with fairy fear. Human. Who would have thought!"

The dining hall suddenly fell silent. Not a sound could be heard, no eating, talking, or plates clattering; all the commotion had stopped. Madame Louise put her head in her hands, unsure if she should have discussed the human issue at all at that moment. Mademoiselle Francesca appearing in front of their table led her to believe she was right; she should not have mentioned the human child at all in the dining hall!

Gasp after gasp circulated through the room. *Humans! Human child? Did they see a human?* Mademoiselle Francesca turned and faced the curious crowd. Not once raising her voice, she firmly instructed everyone to continue what they were supposed to be doing. Though plates clattered and silverware did clink and rattle against each other, voices were but a whisper.

Mademoiselle Francesca sat down with Madame Louise and Pearle. She took a bite of her scone, complete with cream and jelly, savored the taste, and washed it down with a sip of rosehip tea. Sensing Madame Louise thought she had caused a disruption, she quickly put her mind at ease.

"Our run-in with Ellie couldn't have possibly been contained." She took another sip of hot rosehip tea and set the teacup down on the saucer. "By now, the boys will have told everyone in their dorm and, mark my words, the story will soon spread like wildfire."

"What should we do?" Madame Louise whispered. "It could get out of hand very quickly."

Mademoiselle Francesca nodded; she agreed.

"The elders will call an emergency assembly to discuss this issue. They'll determine at that time what, if anything, we do."

Mademoiselle was right. It didn't take long before fairy after fairy came up to the boys' table and asked Boris and Jack to tell them the story about the human in the forest. *Funny how the story keeps changing*, thought Mademoiselle. Each time the story was told, Ellie sounded like a monster, a complete nightmare. How on earth had they all survived such a horrific event and lived to talk about it? Crowds gathered around the boys as they excitedly told their version of what had happened. Jack had the floor.

"Massive, absolutely massive, wasn't it Boris?"

"It was," Boris replied. "And loud; the sound that thing made, never heard anything like it before!"

"It could have squashed us all with one swipe of its hand or stepped on us with those enormous feet!" Jack wasn't done. "They called it Ellie. But don't let that nice name fool you; when it opened its mouth and shrieked, it literally shook all of the trees!"

Boris nodded, agreeing with every word that Jack said.

Mademoiselle Francesca, Madame Louise, and Pearle listened to the boys' conversation. Grinning, they noticed that nothing the boys said about sweet Ellie was consistent.

"You should've been there!" Boris stated. "This humongous thing practically attacked us with its distorted face that twisted in a weird way when it was hungry." Suddenly remembering all the treats, Boris added, "And speaking of hungry, it ate every fairy treat that Broderick had prepared for our stinky moss bomb war!"

Madame Louise shook her head as Mademoiselle Francesca pushed Pearle's chariot in between the boys, hoping the gathering would disperse; it didn't work. It became apparent the elders would need to address everyone, sooner rather than later, or panic was sure to set in and spread throughout the mushroom patch.

"Hold on, though, Boris, hold on!" Jack chimed in again. "Don't forget, as humongous as Ellie was, her parents were ten thousand fairy times bigger and were absolutely terrifying!"

"We were scared to bits, and we're not scared of nothing," added Boris. "If I never see another human again, it will be too soon!"

Chapter 19
Emergency Meeting

Whispers echoed through the great 'shroom as everyone waited for Monsieur Monroe, one of the oldest and wisest elders, to begin the emergency meeting. Mademoiselle Francesca, Monsieur Pierre, and several agents, including Agent Chester and Agent Arley, were present. The atmosphere was tense as emotions and anxiety ran high. Humans within proximity to the forest or the colony were never taken lightly, regardless of the circumstance. An actual encounter with fairlings present was a serious issue indeed.

Monsieur Monroe took his position in front of the podium. A quick glance around the room ensured all were present. Lifting a large gavel and slamming it down on the sound block indicated the meeting was officially in progress. The room fell silent as Monsieur Monroe addressed everyone.

"Good evening."

"Good evening, Monsieur," everyone replied in unison.

Monsieur raised his eyebrows, forcing the deep lines embedded in his forehead to wrinkle up. Peering over his round glasses, which had slid down his nose, he shook his head.

"I'm not sure where to start this evening. No point in rehashing what we already know, but we do need to discuss what we're going to do about those humans. Please note it has been confirmed one of our fairlings was in the clutches of one of their young, a child by the name of Ellie." Hesitating, he looked down at the podium. "I am deeply disturbed by this, as I know you are, but I am assured the fairling is well."

Whispers filled the room but were quickly silenced as Monsieur Monroe continued.

"How do we ensure this never happens again?" he asked in a stern voice, adding, "the floor is open."

Agent Arley squirmed in his seat. As a special agent, he felt it was his duty to inform the elders how the fairlings found themselves in the presence of the human child in the first place. It really couldn't have been helped. It was safe to say it was quite by accident that she ended up where she did in the first place, and the fairlings and those escorting them couldn't have possibly prevented the meeting. Agent Arley slowly stood up and made his way to the podium.

"Monsieur, if I may?"

Monsieur nodded; Agent Arley had their attention and all eyes on him. Finding himself at the center of attention made him uncomfortable, but he shrugged it off and focused on the matter at hand.

"It is concerning that I find myself addressing this situation at all."

All around the room, heads nodded in agreement. It was a terrible situation they found themselves in!

"However, that said, I don't believe we're in danger."

Gasps rang out and looks of disapproval started to merge across the faces of his colleagues and peers. Mademoiselle Francesca and Madame Louise listened intently. Agent Arley held up his hands and settled down the room before he continued. A nod and a wink of his eye from his friend and colleague, Chester, assured Agent Arley he was on the right track. Agent Arley continued to choose his words carefully as he delivered his message.

"It was by pure chance the human child, Ellie, stumbled upon our fairlings and those that escorted them. They were far from the colony, participating in one of Boris's famous moss bomb wars." Flashbacks of Boris and moss bombs bulging out of his pockets from his never-ending supply came to mind. "You know how it's been since Boris was granted his wish: nonstop moss bomb wars."

Smiles and grins replaced the fear and disapproval across the faces of those in the room. Boris's moss bombs wars were becoming legendary, and though no elder would admit it in the meeting, they loved to pelt each other with them as well.

"We were escorting the young ones back to the colony when the incident happened. The child had wandered away from her family. Lost. She was lost! You can only imagine how losing one so young would be; do you remember what is was like when our Lilly and Boris were lost?"

As his eyes browsed the room, he noticed heads bobbing up and down, agreeing with him. Losing the young fairlings had consumed them all with a terrible feeling of fear and anxiety. Agent Arley had the confidence to continue.

"Ellie was quite fairling-like, and by that, I mean she was young and innocent, much like our little ones. She was curious, but she wasn't aggressive. For all intents and purposes, despite her size, she was no different than our very own fairies." Both hands holding on to the podium for support, Agent Arley continued to explain.

"The human child, in my opinion and likely those of the elders present at the time, is like our fairlings in more ways than one. Young. Innocent. Dependent on elders, her parents, kindhearted, curious, and more than anything, she was scared when she was alone."

Not a sound could be heard in the 'shroom except the roof creaking as the wind blew. Not sure if those present were shocked, confused, or if they understood what they had just heard, or they simply didn't know what to say. Either way, the room was dead silent. Mademoiselle Francesca softly asked him to proceed. She had been present that evening and knew exactly what he meant. "I agree, Agent Arley. Please continue."

"Ellie, the child, was scared because she was lost, hungry, and tired. Things our fairies, young fairlings, also experience. Though she was curious about our little ones, despite what you've heard, it wasn't in a hostile or negative way." He took a sip of water from a glass sitting next to the podium. It was only after he'd swallowed that he wondered if the water was for him. Talking about the next part could be tricky. How could he put the elders' minds at ease? Agent Arley thought about what he would say before he spoke. The silence was becoming awkward, but he finally spoke again.

"Ellie did have Lilly in her grasp, but she never once hurt her, and Mademoiselle Francesca can confirm that fact for you."

Mademoiselle jumped to her feet and confirmed Agent Arley's claim indeed was true. Lilly hadn't even been afraid of Ellie, though granted, she likely didn't understand the full extent of the danger she could have been in had Ellie squeezed her hand shut.

"Ellie's parents were terrified, but that's because they feared for her safety just as we would be petrified of losing one of our own. A search and rescue party of such a size was launched and drifted so far *only* because the child was lost."

Monsieur Monroe's face relaxed, easing the scrunched-up lines embedded in his forehead. His eyes softened, and in a gentle voice, commanded, "Continue."

Agent Arley stepped out from behind the in front of the podium and walked back and forth as he spoke. His hands were moving up and down as he wrapped up his position, and Mademoiselle Francesca couldn't help but think what an amazing job Agent Arley had done to convince the elders the colony wasn't in danger. Outstanding!

"Based on everything we witnessed, experienced, and what the scouts continue to report, I do not believe our colony is in danger at this time. It goes without saying that we'll always have to be leery of humans entering this side of the forest, and if they try to build and never leave, well, we'll have to discuss relocating the colony at that time to avoid potential danger. In my opinion, as a guard of our security, I do not believe the humans have any reason to drift so far north any time soon, if ever again, since it was the child they were seeking. Still, the security measures we have in place will continue."

Clasping his hands behind his back, Agent Arley lowered his head and stared at his feet. He took a deep breath and delivered his last piece of advice to the elders.

"I speak for my colleagues and myself when I say that, as shocking as this event was at the time, our colony and all who abide here are not in any current danger. Therefore, I strongly suggest we simply stay alert, monitor as usual, and be grateful this turned out the way that it did."

Chapter 20
Something About Ellie

Lilly and her friends gathered in the courtyard to sun themselves in the fresh air. Though no one said a word, they were all thinking about the same thing: Ellie. Bumping into Ellie had been quite terrifying at first, but the experience had left quite an impression on them all. Lilly couldn't stop thinking about the little girl she had played with while in the forest. Distracted, she didn't hear a word her friends were saying around her. When Lilly failed to respond to Ivy's question, Rosie quizzed her to find out if something was wrong with their sweet friend.

"Lilly, are you unwell?" Rosie asked.

Lilly didn't respond.

"Lilly," Rosie snapped sternly. "Are you ill?"

Lilly jumped when she heard her name spoken so firmly and quickly paid attention to her friend. Rosie asked Lilly again if she was unwell. Lilly shook her head; she felt fine.

"It's Ellie. I can't seem to quit thinking about her."

Ivy sat down next to Lilly and placed an arm around Lilly's shoulders.

"I'm sure you're still in shock. Being captured in the palm of her hand like that must have been terrifying."

Rosie and Pearle agreed it must have been awful for Lilly, being trapped in the palm of a human's hand and possibly being squashed at any second, and still singing as if there wasn't anything wrong. Lilly was by far the bravest fairy they knew!

Oddly enough, Lilly hadn't felt as fearful as maybe she should have been. Chatting with Ellie was fun, exciting, and even interesting. Lilly didn't think about being in the palm of a human's hand. Knowing Ellie was lost made Lilly feel sad, and there was something about Ellie that Lilly liked, maybe her kind eyes, laugh, or was it her red bow? Whatever it was, Ellie hadn't scared Lilly at all.

"I think we're more alike than we realize," Lilly muttered. "Ellie laughed, she cried, she liked to sing, and she loved Broderick's treats."

"She did have pretty hair and eyes," Ivy added. "And I did love that big red bow."

"Me too," giggled Lilly. "I have one just like it, though of course not as big, in pink."

The more the girls chatted about Ellie, the more they realized they were more alike than they could have imagined. On the other hand, Ellie's teardrops were so big she could have easily drowned them all.

"Do you think we'll ever meet Ellie again?" Pearle asked.

Lilly thought about the question before she answered. Would Ellie remember them if they did run into each other again? Ellie was lovely, and Lilly didn't mind if one day, far, far away from now, they did meet again. However, Lilly would be quite content if she never ran into Ellie's parents ever again. Grownup humans were terrifying, massive, loud, and dangerous. Finally, Lilly answered Pearle.

"I don't know, but I think for now it might be best for everyone if we didn't run into her any time soon." Lilly hovered next to Pearle's chariot. "I think I'm glad we met Ellie, but I'm delighted she went home."

Lilly caught a glimpse of Chester out of the corner of her eye. He was sitting on the edge of the water fountain in the middle of the courtyard. She had mastered the art of ignoring Chester's presence, as instructed by the elders, but that didn't stop her from smiling when she caught his friendly wink. He was at ease, and Lilly knew this meant all was well in the colony; any threat of humans drifting too close to the mushroom patch had been removed.

"Pearle, may I?" Lilly asked. "My wings are bent, and my feet are killing me."

"Of course you may," Pearle responded, tapping her lap and scooting her chariot over toward her friend.

Boris nudged Jack and pointed to Pearle and Lilly. If he wasn't mistaken, it looked as if the girls were getting ready to Spin a Fairling Green. One of Boris's favorite games. He waited to see if Rosie and Ivy were jumping on board. He was in luck; both girls dove onto Pearle's chariot; Rosie sat on the chair's right arm and Ivy sat on the chair's left arm.

"Let's play Spin a Fairling Green," suggested Pearle.

Lilly searched the courtyard for Boris and Jack. Spotting them, she waved them over. She didn't have to ask them twice. Jack circled the chariot before swooping down and placing himself on the back of the chair. Boris joined him. Wheeling her chariot over to a clear spot in the courtyard, Pearle started the countdown. Knowing what was coming next, everyone held on as tightly as they possibly could. Pearle started spinning slowly at first. It didn't take long, and Pearle started spinning faster and faster. Suddenly their laughter stopped as everyone hung on for dear life. Lilly, turning quite pale, flew off Pearle's lap and sat down in the grass. Her head was still dizzy, and because her legs were wobbly, she didn't dare stand. Rosie, who wasn't quite grey, hung on for a few more seconds before flying off into the dirt. Boris and Jack burst out laughing and continued to hang onto Pearle's spinning chair as if it were nothing. Ivy, though she had stayed on quite a while, looked as if she might throw up. Grey. Ivy was definitely turning a weird shade of grey.

"Jump, Ivy," Jack hollered. "You're turning grey."

Ivy hung on for two more spins but could hold on no longer. Spilling onto the ground, Ivy rolled and rolled down the path before coming to a stop. She grazed her knees but was so glad to be off the spinning chair she didn't mind. Not knowing whether to laugh, cry, or throw up, Ivy put her head in the water fountain to cool off and help stop the dizziness.

"Why do they play this game?" Mademoiselle Francesca asked as she passed through the courtyard.

"I could never," Madame Louise replied. "I have no idea why they think spinning until they're green or throw up is fun!"

As usual, Boris and Jack were the last two holding on; Boris insisted Pearle spin faster. Pearle, who never got sick, laughed, and felt compelled to oblige. Faster and faster she spun her chariot, the entire chair tipping on one side. Jack, though he hung on for dear life, couldn't do it any longer. His face had turned completely green, and he knew if he didn't jump now, he too, would be joining Ivy in the water fountain. Despite trying to outlast Boris, he had no choice but to throw himself off the chariot. Like Ivy, Jack hit the path, but he rolled to the left down a hill. Finally coming to a stop, he tried with all his might to stand up, but being dizzy, he fell down again. Bursts of laugher, a familiar sound, let him know that Boris was enjoying his win. Boris, though truly green, was the last fairy to step off the chariot. Pearle pulled on the brakes and Boris thought he might go flying over her head. Bracing himself, he managed to remain on the chair until Pearle had come to a complete stop. Once again, Boris was the Spin a Fairling Green champion!

"I don't know how you do it, Boris!" Jack laughed. "I tried to stay on, but Pearle was too fast."

"And yet not fast enough for me," Boris chuckled. "Once again, I am the champion!"

Lilly, finding it difficult to walk in a straight line, hovered instead toward the others. Her wings were bent, her stomach was still doing flips, and she desperately wanted some of Broderick's famous ginger-mint tea. If she was lucky, Cook might have some on hand; if not, she'd settle for a hot cup of rosehip tea to settle her tummy. Ivy suggested tea in the courtyard, and everyone agreed that it was a fabulous idea! Boris, Rosie, and Pearle brought a tray filled with tea, fairy biscuits, and hot fairy scones outside as Lilly, Jack, and Ivy tried to recuperate from their game.

"This is lovely, isn't it?" Lilly asked. "Just what I needed."

The fairy friends ate the goodies, drank the tea, and talked about their adventure with Ellie. There was something about Ellie they'd never forget, and even Boris had to admit it was an adventure of a lifetime. Tummies finally settled and color back in their cheeks, they made their way to the dormitories before supper. The girls headed to the left, and the boys to the right; no doubt the bathing room monitor would be expecting them. It was time to take a bath, straighten their wings, and eat their supper before bed. It had been a great day filled with good fairy fun after their wild adventure.

Chapter 21
Surprise

Fairies piled into the assembly hall and took their seats for morning announcements. Monsieur Pierre was having a terrible time confiscating stinky moss bombs as they flew through the air. If only removing Boris from the hall would eliminate the problem, but it wouldn't. He had learned that Boris and Jack had become quite proficient at moss bomb trade and had accumulated enough marbles, fairy twists, conkers, and suckers to start trading those items as well. It seemed everyone was well stocked with stinky, slimy moss bombs. The moss bomb problem had gone beyond Boris and Jack and was, as the elders feared, colony-wide! Regularly scheduled battles would become a priority to keep the moss bombs out of the class 'shrooms.

Lilly found an empty seat and sat down next to Boris. A glance upward revealed Chester sitting in the rafters in his usual spot, third beam directly overhead above her. Lilly thought she might never understand why she had received such a gift, the ability to see special agents while others couldn't, but knowing Chester was always around had become a comfort to her. Chester pointed toward the aisle; Rosie was looking for her friends. Lilly stood up and waived, and as soon as Rosie spotted her, she grabbed Ivy and found empty seats in Lilly's row. Pearle parked her chariot in the back of the hall but still had a great view of the stage. All the elders were seated up front, and as soon as they stood up, the fairlings knew it was time to stop talking, stand up until told to be seated, and pay attention to the announcements.

Monsieur Pierre approached the podium and introduced Agent Byford. Agent Byford greeted everyone and delivered an encouraging message.

"There have been whisperings about strangers in the forest, but I can assure you there is no need to be afraid. We must always be on guard, this is true, but the immediate threat is no longer present."

Agent Byford looked around the room; all eyes were upon him, and he knew he had their attention. Clearly, the humans had been on everyone's mind.

"The humans are nowhere near our colony, and it's safe to say the threat has been removed. You may go about your business as you normally would, with the comfort of knowing you are safe."

Applause broke out in the assembly hall, but once Monsieur Pierre stood up, the clapping and cheers died down, and Agent Byford took a seat. Monsieur Pierre introduced Mademoiselle Francesca, who was, as always, the picture of perfection to Lilly. Her bun was neat and tidy, she didn't have a single wrinkle in her dress, and her rosy cheeks complimented her bright blue eyes. Lilly beamed when Mademoiselle's eyes met hers, and Mademoiselle gave her a fairy wink. Mademoiselle was her favorite elder, and Lilly couldn't wait to be just like her one day. Greeting everyone with a lovely big smile, Mademoiselle Francesca addressed the assembly.

"My, what an adventure several of you experienced!" She smiled and looked around the room. "But now it is time to get back to reality. Lessons. Homework. Oh, and what else was it? Ah, that's right. We must prepare for our fairy ball."

Mademoiselle Francesca hushed the squeals of excitement that rippled through the hall. Fairy ball! There was going to be a fairy ball?!

"You have not been dismissed, and I am not done. Where are your manners?" Mademoiselle smiled, knowing how excited everyone was about the ball. "There is much work and planning to do. I'll post a list of all the committees that we need by the end of the week. I would like it very much if each one of you would all sign up for a committee and join in the fun."

Madame Louise suddenly appeared next to Mademoiselle Francesca. Gasps filled the room; she looked just like a fairy princess. Lilly had never seen such a beautiful fairy in all her life. Madame Louise's gown was long, trailing the ground, and had multiple layers that made it full and fluffy. It was a shade of lilac that Lilly had never seen, trimmed in silver, and laced with sparkling jewels. Mademoiselle Francesca held Madame Louise's hand so she could twirl for the fairies, especially the girls. Monsieur Claude suddenly appeared next to her. He looked very handsome! Wearing posh clothes that Boris and Jack had only seen a few times before, and suddenly Boris and Jack panicked. They knew where this was going, and they didn't like it, not one little bit! Were they going to have to dress like that too? Boris didn't pull off fancy attire very well. The fairies looked on in wonder and oohed and aahed over Madame Louise and Monsieur Claude's attire. Boris and Jack thought Monsieur Claude looked ridiculous.

"He looks like he can't move!"

"You know what this means, don't you?" Boris asked Jack, scared to death. "They'll want us to dress like that; I'll look like him—ridiculous."

Mademoiselle Francesca raised her hand, and everyone stopped talking. The fairy ball would take place within two full moons. It would be a magnificent ball, one that everyone could take part in and enjoy. Preparing for the ball and planning was half the fun and being part of a committee would build friendship bonds and teach the fairlings how to work together to get things done. Everyone was excited about the ball, except for Boris and Jack. They didn't want to be on a committee, and they certainly didn't want to go to the ball!

Madame Louise, as excited about the ball as the fairies were, could hardly contain herself. She already had her dress, and it couldn't be more perfect! Standing at the podium, Madame Louise reminded everyone to choose their committee carefully. After all, they'd be working together with those on the committee for some time and representing everyone in their colony. Monsieur Pierre whispered in Mademoiselle Francesca's ear. Nodding, Mademoiselle directed Monsieur to the podium.

"This is exciting, isn't it?" he asked, already knowing the answer.

Cheers broke out around the hall, but Boris and Jack were not impressed. From stinky moss bomb wars to fairy balls; how on earth did this happen?! The elders had one more special announcement, and Monsieur Pierre couldn't wait to share the news.

"We've arranged for Monsieur Marcel, from the Northwest Colony, to join us."

Everyone sat in silence, unsure who that was, or what they were supposed to say. As soon as Monsieur Pierre realized he had gotten ahead of himself, he mopped his brow with his handkerchief, belly laughed, and explained to the fairies exactly who Monsieur Marcel happened to be.

"He's a renowned dance instructor, and each one of you will learn how to fairy quadrille and fairy waltz.'

"What?!" cried Boris. "A fairy what?"

"This is terrible," added Jack. "Absolutely terrible!"

Monsieur Pierre took Mademoiselle Francesca's hand in his, twirled her around, and took two long floaty strides forward. Mademoiselle followed with ease and then, of all things, they took several more steps in sets of twos and twirled around the stage. Lilly and her friends, too excited to sit still, clapped and cheered as Mademoiselle and Monsieur danced. They looked beautiful and, of all things, she and her friends would be wearing beautiful gowns and learning how to dance just like that soon enough; how exciting!

They dismissed the fairies, and chatter filled the halls. Lilly, too excited to concentrate on her next lesson, sent word to her friends. *Let's meet in the fairy garden as soon as we're dismissed and figure out what committee we'd like to join.* Everyone except for Boris and Jack agreed. Committee, forget it, they'd dodge Lilly and their friends and think of something else to do instead. How on earth could this happen?

About the Author

Amanda M. Thrasher was born in England, moved to Texas, and resides there still. She's an award-winning author of Young Adult, General Fiction, Middle Grade, Early Reader Chapter, and Picture Books. Amanda is a multiple Gold Recipient of The Mom's Choice Awards® (MCA), earning the award in multiple categories, including Young Adult, General Fiction, and Early Reader Chapter Books. She is also a two-time Gold Medal winner of the Readers' Favorite International Book awards, a New Apple Literary Award winner, and a North Texas Book Festival award winner. Visit Amanda's website at **amandamthrasher.com.**

Amanda founded and is the CEO of Progressive Rising Phoenix Press, an independent publishing company. She shares her writing and publishing experience with others through school visits, book signings, trade conferences, and workshops for aspiring writers of all ages.

In addition, Amanda was contracted to write a graphic novel for the Driving on the Right Side of the Road Program. The publication is part of the Driving on the Right Side of the Road (DRSR) program, developed by the Law-Related Education Department of the State Bar of Texas Law Focused Education, Inc. and the Texas Municipal Courts Education Center with funding from the Texas Court of Criminal Appeals and the Texas Department of Transportation. The program's purpose is to offer a preventive educational program to encourage responsible decision-making when it comes to obeying traffic laws and following safe practices. The graphic novel, titled *What If ... A Story of Shattered Lives,* was adapted into a reader's theater for as few as five speakers or as many as twenty-six and remains part of the DRSR program.

Progressive Rising Phoenix Press is an independent publisher. We offer wholesale pricing and multiple binding options with no minimum purchases for schools, libraries, book clubs, and retail vendors. We offer substantial discounts on bulk orders and discounts on individual sales through our online store. Please visit our website at:

www.ProgressiveRisingPhoenix.com

If you enjoyed reading this book, please review it on

Amazon, B & N, or Goodreads. Thank you in advance!